Just Hit SEND

A Journey to Freedom

Jody Vehr

PUBLISHED BY TAJJ IMPRINTS

Just Hit Send: A Journey to Freedom
Jody Vehr
Copyright © 2015 by Jody Vehr

Publisher:
Tajj Imprints
2020 W. Quail Ave.
Phoenix AZ 85027

Cover art: *A Tribute To My Coach* courtesy, Briggs Whiteford
Cover Design: Carrie Brito
Book Interior Design: Chris Molé

ISBN: 978-0-9967068-0-3

First Edition
9 8 7 6 5 4 3 2 1

This book is dedicated to YOU.
Yes, YOU, the beautiful being
holding this book in your hands.
May your life be blessed and
forever changed in the direction
you wish to go.

Contents

Allies & Mentors

Learning to Fly

Foreword

Love in all the wrong places.

The hit country song really struck a nerve when it sang about *looking for love in all the wrong places.*

Most people can relate and identify with the mistakes they made and the wild rides they took while searching for love and approval outside themselves.

Very few people wake up from that nightmare. Most who do, don't say much about it, because there is so much shame and guilt that accompanies being a fool for what looks like love.

Fortunately for you and me, and all the other lucky readers of this wild ride of a book, Jody Vehr has chosen to tell her whole story. And her story is captivating on so many levels.

One could read it shallowly as a romance novel full of raw visceral emotions, brutal psychological abuse and dramatic betrayals. On that level alone, the book is an immediate success … a stay-up-late page-turner. And Jody Vehr is a very gifted storyteller with an entertaining flair for recreating spicy dialogue.

But there is another, deeper level at work in this book from the very beginning. Right at the start, when Jody is a little girl, and her dear dog Kisher dies. Right then you know that this book is going to be different, unlike anything you have ever read. There is a spiritual dimension to this book that will stun you. And even better, as Jody says in the beginning, the spiritual awakenings that she experienced on her journey out of hell are available to all of us.

This book can be a wake-up call to that possibility.

Jody Vehr spares no one in this book, least of all herself. It's trendy now in the self-help world to trumpet praise for "vulnerability." It's suddenly cool to be vulnerable. And while social media and personal transformation gurus are praising vulnerability day and night, who is really showing it to us? To most of its advocates, it's merely an exciting and trendy concept.

To Jody it is startlingly real, poured across every page of this book. Each terrifying emotion that arises in her is ours to see.

We all kind of agree that it's not a good idea to look for love in all the wrong places, and to try to find someone outside yourself who will make you happy, but that's just an idea we agree with. It's conceptual.

The fierce beauty of this book is that it's not conceptual, it's experiential. It's really happening and we are looking, page after page, into a very open heart.

I won't spoil the story's turning point. And unlike most nonfiction books with a spiritual and psychological message, this one really is a story you can't put down. The lessons here are profound. The hero's journey this brave woman makes is also profound. Unforgettable is the word I'd choose if I had to use a single word to describe the book.

My second choice would be the word "useful." This is a book you can use. As a mirror, almost. That's how I used it. To reflect. Where am I missing the divine love that is already inside me by looking for approval and appreciation from others outside of me? When will I ever wake up?

Thanks to Jody Vehr, waking up just got easier to do.

STEVE CHANDLER
Phoenix, Arizona 2015

The Dark Forest

Are you ready to embark on an
extraordinary journey?
In the pages to come is a miraculous story
of the power of love.
And the brilliance of the human spirit.
This story is about YOU.

CHAPTER 1

A new definition of "crisis"

A golf cart?!
Heck no, I'm not arriving to my wedding in a golf cart. I am standing barefoot outside the bridal suite surrounded by iridescent desert red rock beaming down from all angles. The crisp winter air sends a chill from my head to my toes. I watch as everyone is in a hustle and a bustle to get down to Enchantment Circle where I am to marry the love of my life.

My sister is trying to gather up four flower girls who have jumped out of the 1934 Ford Bonnie and Clyde car that has just broken down. They seem more like wild kittens at the moment rather than children. They are running in all directions in confused excitement. I smile finding the moment joyful, even though I am teetering on being late to my own wedding! My ten-year-old niece Ella quickly comes to my side and is tugging on my wedding dress.

"Auntie Jody ... "

I look down to see her glowing sweet face beaming up at me.

"Yes, honey?" I smile and from the corner of my eye see her twin sister Zoe is quickly joining us from across the parking lot. Given the nature of their world, their attentiveness tells me this must be serious stuff.

I kneel down to meet them face-to-face. Their eyes are filled with pure love and concern. Ella continues, "Auntie Jody, you know what? It's not an official wedding until there is a crisis."

I can't help but giggle. Zoe, now at my side, chimes in too. "Yeah, Auntie Jody there always has to be a crisis to make it an official wedding."

Their genuine heart is endearing. Given my life up to this point, I wouldn't consider this quite a crisis, but then again the 1934 Ford my soon-to-be husband bought as a surprise just for the occasion *has* broken down. Definitely not an ideal situation. Especially since he and 125 guests plus the groomsmen are patiently awaiting my arrival.

I give my nieces a big hug, acknowledging their concern. "You know, I actually didn't know every wedding needed a crisis to be official. Thank you so much for sharing this with me. Then I guess the car breaking down is a *good* thing." I give them a little wink and rise again, coming eye to eye with my dad who has seemed to appear out of nowhere.

"Geez Dad, are you Superman or something?" He laughs a short-lived laugh. "We need to get down there honey. I promised your soon to be hubby I would have you to him by 12:12 p.m. That was the deal, 12.12.12 at 12:12 p.m."

This is the happiest day of my life even with "the crisis."

The first golf cart zooms off to the circle taking a couple of flower girls and bridesmaids. I have a few moments until they return for me. Tears of joy sting my eyes as I reflect on the miraculous journey to get here. Images similar to that of a movie screen flash before my mind as I recall the moments of chaos I have walked through, the heartache of betrayal I have healed from, and the courage it took to receive the magnificent experience of awakening to who I truly am.

I see clearly what I once considered tremendous hardship has been a blessing and not a curse. Even in the darkest hour when it seemed I was destined to doom, I see I was being groomed for the greatness of life today.

I am not a religious person by any stretch of the imagination, yet I do know I am guided by a source higher than myself. If one were to look from a higher altitude at my life, it would be obvious by the synchronicity of events that have brought me to where I am. I have gone through the dark night of the soul, taken a full journey through the forest of (real) crisis and confusion, landing in freedom and connection to spirit. I know anyone and everyone can have this connection to Source, which is why I am inspired to tell my story.

I believe as children we all come into life already aware of our connection to a higher power. As the poet Wordsworth said, we come into this world "... trailing clouds of glory." I know it was true for me.

Then something happened.

I remember the exact moment when things shifted and the confusion of humanness set in.

It was at around age seven when my dog Kisher died.

CHAPTER 2

Touched by the angels

Our birth is but a sleep and a forgetting:
The Soul that rises with us, our life's Star,
Hath had elsewhere its setting,
And cometh from afar

~ William Wordsworth

As a very small child I would get visitations from angels. Sometimes they would come when I was in my room lying on my canopy bed playing with my dolls. Other times they would appear at night when I was about to head off into dreamland.

Their energy was warm, safe, and inviting, nurturing in ways similar to a mother's sweet touch or loving embrace. They would sing the most beautiful songs I have ever heard. Their melody comforted my soul in a way that reminded me of where I am from.

As I mentioned, I am not "religious" by any stretch of the imagination. But my early childhood was a spiritual experience much like that of the great poet William Wordsworth as he described it in his *Ode: Intimations of Immortality*. He said we don't come into this world completely naked and unmindful of our origin, but we come trailing clouds of glory, "from God, who is our home. Heaven lies about us in our infancy!"

That was my experience, too. The angels would share stories that only my soul could recognize. I knew their energy and their presence just as I know the energy and presence of a dear friend or family member.

In early childhood I had no question that they were real. They were my family and I knew that without a doubt. There wasn't a barrier between my family in physical life and my family of Spirit. To me, we were all one. Their unending love and radiance filled me with an abounding joy. They were a natural part of life and I assumed everyone had angel friends!

At around age seven, everything changed.

The adults in my life starting suggesting, verbally and non-verbally, it was *all* my over-active imagination. I remember the exact moment I bought into that false belief. It was when my dog Kisher died.

I can flash back to the event like it was yesterday.

It's the night she has been put to sleep. I am lying in my canopy bed crying and feeling devastated. I have just lost one of my best friends. My mom and dad have come to tuck me into bed.

"Jody, it's going to be okay." My mom is wiping the tear stains off my cheek. I pull the covers over my face, just leaving my eyes to show. I give her a tearful hopeless look. My mom is having a hard time fighting back her tears. My dad reaches over and gently squeezes both our arms. "It's really going to be okay honey."

They both give me a few more hugs and kisses before getting up to leave the room. They stand by the door to make sure I am okay. I surprisingly drift off to sleep quickly. Then, all of a sudden, in a half-awake state, I *hear her* at the back door! I pop up in bed like a lightning bolt. *I am so excited! I knew she wasn't gone.*

I plop my little feet on the floor and quietly crawl out of bed. The house is dark so I know that means everyone is asleep. I don't want to wake anyone. I tiptoe to my bedroom door with my little heart beating fast. I gently walk on the tips of my toes through the kitchen. I reach my little hand up the wall to turn the light switch on so I can see my way to the back door. I finally make it and there she is!! I am SO happy! There is my beautiful white fluffy Samoyed! I am shocked to see her glowing with iridescent brilliance ... I take notice right away that her glow isn't from her natural color. She looks transparent like a soft white light bulb. I slowly open the door and let her in. She is wagging her tail something fierce in pure delight! I kneel down and hug her. She almost knocks me over in excitement, giving kisses and licks to my face.

I am ecstatic to see Kisher! But I am also trying to hush her up so my parents won't wake up! I am sure if they do they will take her back to that mean vet who will threaten to put her to sleep again. (Whatever the phrase "putting to sleep" means, I know I didn't like it! It took my Kisher away!)

I begin tiptoeing back to my room, softly calling to her. "Kisher, come on. Come on Kisher." She finally runs and joins me as I crawl back into bed. I am so happy! "How cool is this?!" My parents have never let Kisher into my bed.

She plops onto her side cuddling as close as she can. I feel safe and happy as her breathing tickles my neck. I wrap my arms around her neck burying my face in right by her ear and whisper, "Don't ever leave me again, Kisher." She licks my face as if she's acknowledging me. It feels so wonderful to hold her. I caress her soft fur, holding her neck in my arms. She has a smell that I love. I keep my face buried in her neck, breathing her in with all my might. She lets out a relaxing sigh, nuzzling deeply into my arms.

We peacefully fall asleep together.

The next morning comes quickly. I open my eyes to see my mom sitting on the edge of the bed. She is stroking my hair looking down at me with love and concern.

"Where is Kisher, Mommy?"

My mom's eyes are gentle and concerned. "Kisher's *gone*, Honey."

With that, my little seven-year-old body bolts up in protest. I begin anxiously scanning the room.

"No, she's not Mommy! She was here with me all night! Where is she?!"

My mom tries a loving response to soothe me. "Honey, that was only a dream. It was only in your imagination that she was here."

I continue to look around the room for Kisher in disbelief. I begin to panic that she's really gone. I scan the room and she is nowhere in sight. My heart sinks.

Right here, poof! Reality drastically changes. In this moment, everything shifts. I buy into the false belief that my mom's words of well-intended support are *truth*. My spiritual eyes slowly close, fading to black. My direct knowing of being a spiritual being having a human experience comes to a screeching halt and the journey of humanness begins.

Lying here with my seven-year-old world turned upside down, I have no idea how wild this journey is going to be.

CHAPTER 3

My own personal doomsday

May 6th, 2007: Doomsday.

That's the day the spiritual sledgehammer came swinging down, knocking me off my path so hard I landed face-first into an unexpected sea of utter chaos, chaos I would not wish on my worst enemy.

You know the saying "God doesn't give you more than you can handle?" I came up-close and personal to reaching maximum capacity.

Let me set the scene for you: It's 6:00 a.m. and I am lying in bed half-asleep. I am trying to muster up enough energy to get up and face yet another day. Life is challenging as I am attempting to keep afloat a more-than-rocky relationship. I am living life in a downward spiral with increasingly depleted energy as the norm.

In through the bedroom door comes Wade, my fiancé.

I am startled, since the only interaction we have these days is comprised of horrific fighting. My mind begins to race as my body tenses in protection. "Oh God, here he comes again to have another nasty go around. I can't handle that right now." I pull the covers closer to my face figuring he's about to yell.

Instead, he is handing me the phone.

"It's Artemis," he says. Artemis is a dear friend of mine.

What? It's so early. My mind is spinning and becomes confused. Still cowering a bit, I pull the covers away from my face to turn to look up at Wade. "It's six in the morning," I say to him sleepily. My body goes further into a protective posture as he continues to gesture the phone toward me. He's a tad unpredictable these days so I am trying to avoid talking with him at all costs. "Why is she calling so early?" I stare at the white cordless phone being pushed into my face.

Wade doesn't move. "You're going to want to take this." He gestures once again to the phone, more urgently this time. Anxiety begins to build in my body. It's never a good thing when someone calls at 6:00 a.m. I reach for the phone and crawl out of bed trying to make sense of what is going on. Wade conveniently disappears into the bathroom to take a shower. It's not his forté to support the emotional nature of things.

I groggily walk down the hallway, phone to ear, taking notice that the sun is just beginning to come up over the lake. A mist of fog is kissing the water with hundreds of Canadian geese greeting the day in serenade.

I skip over hello. "What's going on Arte?"

As I begin to listen to her speak my world begins to shake.

"Jody, something awful has happened." Her words send a chill to my core. She begins to sob, muttering something I cannot understand.

"Slow down, Arte. Tell me what's going on." There is a deafening pause on the other end.

"It's DJ," she blurts out, her cadence unforgiving. "He's dead, Jody. He died of a massive heart attack last night."

I lose my breath as if someone just punched me in the chest. All the walls around me are beginning to cave in. Her words pierce my soul like a knife to the heart. Tremendous panic overtakes me in a wave of utter chaos. I become consumed by fear and disbelief. The world is shaking from the ground to my head. Everything I know is crumbling and crashing around me. I begin to lose it in a way that defines whether one has inner strength or not. I can hardly hold the phone in my hand. My breath continues to fail me as I grapple for some sort of control. My ego reaches for logic. *Is she joking? Am I dreaming? What the hell is going on?*

The sobbing on the other end of the phone tells me this is not a joke. I lose what little control I have as full-blown shock sets in. Tears begin to come to the surface from a place deeper than I have ever known.

"What are you saying to me Arte? This is not funny. What are you saying to me?!" I feel as if I am pleading with God. But blown reality begins to sink in.

"OH MY GOD!" I can no longer hold to reason. I burst into tears, falling to my knees. "No, no, no!"

I am completely outside my body, feeling as if someone just ripped my heart out and handed it back to me saying, "Have fun with this one!" I drop the phone and curl up into a ball unable to do anything but feel and cry. As I lay here time becomes nonexistent. I can hear Arte calling to me through the phone but I am unable to reach for it. With every ounce of my being I grapple with *how is this possible?*

I have never experienced such excruciating pain as I did in that moment. Time stopped. Everything came to a screeching halt and there I lay, on the floor, the phone plopped next to my hand, begging my friend to tell me it is not so. It hurt unlike any hurt I had ever known.

That is, unlike any hurt I had ever known until three days later.

That's when my entire world and everything I believed in, including myself, was turned upside down and inside out. The next three days are three days that will test my spirit and define who I will become.

CHAPTER 4

The night the shadow beckoned

Daryl Joe Swalosdayle. A strange name indeed, but well suited for the strange-but-true story that's about to be told.

In my world, Daryl Joe, known to most as DJ, was the closest person to me. I adored him with my heart and soul.

He was even closer to me than my fiancé, Wade.

But little did I know that DJ was not who he portrayed himself to be. What was to come was shocking beyond my wildest imagination.

For the last six years, prior to his passing, I studied American shamanism with him. In my mind, he was my beloved and trusted teacher. We were bonded by what seemed to be a shared love of spirituality and a genuine interest in the healing and growth of the human spirit. I cherished studying with him and considered it a life-saving experience.

Prior to landing in his universe in 2001 at the age of twenty-eight, I'd been recklessly running in the world of drugs and raving. I pushed things to the extreme; slamming my mind, body, and soul straight into the ground, landing in a puddle of disconnection with little to no self-esteem. By the time I arrived in his world I was hanging by a thread to a shattered sense of reality.

I can vividly recall how studying with him came to be.

Rewind to shortly after the New Year in 2001. Things in my life are way out of control. I am sitting in my bedroom amidst a drug-induced emotional breakdown. Not knowing what else to do, I grab for a piece of paper that has been sitting in my desk drawer for the last couple of years with DJ's number handwritten on it. My friend Artemis, who has studied with him for over ten years, gave it to me awhile back urging me to contact him, knowing full well of my downward spiral.

I now know it's time to make a desperate phone call to DJ's assistant and co-teacher. I need to find out if there happens to be a class starting soon. I fumble with the phone and dial the number, trembling. The ring on the other side seems to have a long echo. Finally someone picks up.

"Hello?" It's a female voice so I assume it's his assistant Nicole. "Hi, is this Nicole?

"Yes it is."

"Hi Nicole, this is Jody, I spoke to you a couple of years ago by way of my friend Artemis …"

Artemis had coordinated an introductory event, but at that point I had no interest in studying with DJ.

"Ah, yes Jody, how are you?" There is a tone in her voice that seems to know why I am calling.

"I'm not doing so well." My voice trembles as I begin to stumble with the embarrassment and shame of my desperation. I continue anyway. "Well, so, I am calling to see if there happens to be a class starting sometime soon?"

I know my broken state is obvious but at this point I don't care. There is a slight rustle of a muffled phone on her end followed by a few seconds of pause. She comes back with a response. "Well actually Jody there is a class starting this weekend and we have one spot left." Her words send an odd mixture of relief and resistance. "Would you like to join us?

If so, you can bring your deposit with you and make payments on the rest."

Even though I am financially broke and reluctant, given my current state of dysfunction I agree to attend. I know deep down the alternative is worse, and quite possibly a path to destruction. An agreement is made for me to be there.

Like a dream, the next few days fly by. It seems suddenly I am walking out of my apartment, heading into a direction unknown. As I close the door I take immediate notice of the biting chill in the air. The Bay Area fog is rolling in with a certain vengeance. I pull my hoodie over my head, drawing it even tighter to my chest in an attempt to keep warm. I clench my overnight bag with my other hand and walk across the street to my car. I've packed light for once, my journal being the most important item.

Finally I'm out of the city, humming along on the freeway on a four-hour drive north from San Francisco to Grass Valley where DJ lives and conducts his classes. I try to keep my nervousness at bay by occupying myself with rhythmic beats of music thumping through the car speakers. Time flies while in a half-meditative state.

As I get off the freeway and twist and turn on the roads toward his house, the quasi-surreal energy fades. *Holy crap! What am I doing?!* My heart begins to beat fast and loud. Inching down the final mountain road to his home, I watch the addresses on the sign posts grow closer to his. A full-blown panic attack begins to set in. I hear a faint loving voice within whispering to me, "Take a deep breath, Sweet Angel."

I am startled by the voice, for I have no idea where it came from or what that is. I ignore it. I am completely consumed and preoccupied with the fact I have now found his driveway. I pull in with a full-blown anxiety attack in effect. *What is my problem?* The anxiety seems to be unfounded. I stop the car at the end of the driveway. I open the door slowly, step out, and begin walking toward his house, feeling as if I am hobbling to the front doorstep, broken in spirit. From the drugs I have done at the raves I am completely confused about what is real, which way is up, and how I am ever going to heal from the marathon I have just run on a battlefield of darkness. I have seen and experienced things that not even the most articulate journalist could describe. And, that's a good thing.

DJ opens the door before I get to it.

"Hello, Jody, it's nice to see you."

I look up, meeting his eyes. A chill runs along my neck.

In this moment, with his beaming blue eyes and welcoming smile, he becomes the light in the dark, the only way out for me. I somehow, unexplainably, feel an instant trust for him, which further sets the stage for him as the sole lifeline from the chaotic life I live. Over time, he will become everything to me.

So, as you may see, in current reality wrapping my mind around him being gone is similar to trying to wrap my mind around the very nature of eternity.

It's not happening. I am unable to comprehend how it is, the man I trusted and loved with all my heart and soul, is POOF, gone! All in an unknown instant.

I have lost others in life. When it happened I knew the moment they passed. I felt it by way of our connection. But in this case, I did not sense a thing. Not even a flutter of energy. Very strange indeed.

Yes, I know, shock is a natural reaction to losing someone we love … especially to losing someone who is our spiritual teacher, right? Absolutely.

But there is more to this story. Way more.

It's eight months into studying with DJ, and it's been life changing. No more drugs. No nasty boyfriend anymore. I've slowed life way down to where I am getting the much overdue time I've needed in order to truly heal. I think it's smooth sailing from here, but actually I'm headed toward a world that's turned inside out and upside down.

Tonight, at first wind, the shadow beckons my soul.

It's our monthly class and we're headed into nature to spend time on a remote lake for the weekend. Artemis is standing next to me in DJ's driveway helping to pack up the cars so we can get on our way. I turn to her in excitement, "I am thrilled our camping trip is here! I love studying this Shamanism stuff! Thanks for introducing this to me, Arte."

She gives me one of her lovely smiles. "I am honored to have made the introduction between you and DJ." She has seen my growth and I know she is thankful for it.

We're finally at the lake! We wasted little time setting up camp so we could enjoy the day. It's a scorching hot September afternoon. We just arrived back from our first outing on the water. As DJ pulls the boat up to the shore we all jump out into knee high water. He is beside me as I reach in to grab my backpack. "Having a good time, Jo?" He is securing the boat from drifting by tying it to an anchor of some sort.

"Yes! I am having a fantastic time!" My excitement is obvious. I am beaming. I give him a childlike smile and begin heading up to camp.

I just adore DJ.

He's like a father to me. Over the last eight months his kindness, wisdom, and support have brought a new level of confidence to my world. For the first time I know I am on the right path. I have never trusted another in the way I trust him. I trust him wholeheartedly. The best part is I even feel I trust myself, which is a miraculous first in my life.

As I walk to camp my thoughts are lighthearted. I am floating around in what my friends jokingly call the "Jody World." I am thinking to myself, "Thank goodness he came into my life, I don't know where I'd be without him. Everyone should have a teacher like him."

The day continues on to be gorgeous. The sun is bright in the vibrant blue sky. White clouds kiss the landscape in a scattered cottonball brilliance. With a little free time I fly solo to stand on top of a hill looking out over the lake. I watch as a witness to the sun dancing on top of the ripples as if there is no other way for it to be. The sparkles light up as if thousands of angels are before me. I close my eyes, take in a deep long breath and let it *all* go. I notice a gentle cool breeze caressing my face offering the first signs of fall. I am so thankful I am twenty-eight and finally figured things out. I feel at peace for the first time in my life. The bumpy path of the past seems to have changed into smooth sailing.

"Looking forward to our fire circle tonight?" DJ startles me from behind grabbing my sides in a playful gesture that jolts me out of my peaceful daydream. He is always affectionate with us. Something I have come to treasure. It has somehow assisted in healing my abusive past where men were not always so kind and loving to me.

"I sure am! I am really looking forward to the trance process we are going to do tonight."

Part of our work together is going into guided meditation to meet with our Spirit Guides, or Teachers, as he calls them. This one in particular is for giving ourselves permission to keep our secrets.

The sun has set and we have gathered around the fire circle. It is crackling and flickering in a way that is mesmerizing to the soul. As I listen to the popping fizzle of the warm flames I settle in for our journey inward. I am wrapped in a cozy blanket, with my hoodie pulled over my head. I am nuzzled in my chair, ready to go. I am awaiting DJ's familiar closed-eye countdown to inner space.

DJ always encourages the group to smoke pot before going into trance. He says it helps loosen us up. Except for rare occasions, I always refuse. Given my past with drugs, I don't want anything to hinder my connection to Spirit. Tonight is no exception. I choose to defer and go the sober route.

He senses we are set. With a soothing tone he begins, "Okay now, take a few deep breaths in and let it all go … " I am accustomed to the sound of his voice and have no problem surrendering to my inner sanctuary. "Go deep into your space. I am going to count you back from ten and when I reach one you will be there" He pauses. "Ten, nine, eight …"

We travel, and by the count of one we are there, in our inner sanctuary.

"That's it," he says. "Now get yourself acclimated … There you go … " We spend the next hour guided by his monologue. Much of the details are a blur to me. I only hear that I now have the right to create a space for secrets.

"Now you will begin to come back …" I begin to drift away from inner space coming back to current reality. "I will count backwards from ten and once I reach one you will be fully present. "Ten, nine, eight …" I begin to hear the crackling of the fire next to me. We reach one. I slowly open my eyes and try to come back into my body. "Wow," I think. "What a journey that was."

We spend a little time bundled together around the fire sharing our experiences. The conversation naturally winds down and is complete. We are all beaming, in a great space, ready to spend a little time in R & R.

"Woo hoo!" I think, "It's off duty time!"

Off duty time is when we get to hang out and share our friendship and kinship. I walk over to the ice chest. Arte joins me.

"I love you," she says. "I am so happy we are on this journey together."

"Me too, I love you too, Arte." We grab a drink and walk back over to the fire. I sit down next to DJ who is busy talking to another classmate. Arte takes a seat next to me and together we sit in silence as we watch as the fire casts playful dancing shadows across our faces. It's a new moon, so it's especially dark outside. The stars above twinkle with a magic that calls the mystic out of me. I lay my head back on my chair in contemplation and think to myself, "How is it that I cannot comprehend *forever* with my mind but here I can look up into the night sky and see it?"

Then I feel a squeeze on my right hand.

I whirl around to my right and see it's DJ, who is still sitting in the chair next to me.

It's extremely dark and hard to see but I give him a smile and a squeeze back intending to let go immediately. I am trying to pull my hand away but he continues to hold on tight. I begin to sense something is off. Oh my gosh, this is weird. Confusion begins to set in as my stomach drops.

Given the fact I have NO self-esteem and I have placed him on a God pedestal, trusting his every word, I find I am unable to tell him how awkward and uncomfortable this is. My mind is racing. *What is he doing?!* I feel as if my hand is dead weight. It's becoming painfully clear his intention is not merely a friendly gesture of affection.

Panic begins to creep in. The foundation of innocence I've placed DJ in is beginning to shake and become unstable. All the trust and confidence I once felt begins to crumble. My heart is beginning to pound. I feel as if it is thumping a beat the whole way up to my ears. I am really uncomfortable with what is going on.

Flashes of my past begin to come to the surface—flashes of acts of dishonor from others where I felt I had no way out. This is becoming so uncomfortable I abruptly pull my hand from his and excuse myself to go away to sleep.

I address my classmates. "I'm tired and going to head to the tent and get some shut-eye. I'll see you all in the morning." Everyone says good night to me, sending me their, "I love you's"

But sleep is the furthest thing from my mind. I don't know what else to do but to go hide out in my tent. Anxiety is an understatement for what's going on.

"Goodnight Jo," he says in an odd way that sends me over the edge. His energy reminds me of a predator playing with its soon-to-be-killed prey. I mutter a half goodnight, not even looking at him. I walk to my tent with my heart beating faster than I have ever thought possible. My breath is shallow. I am shaking, worried, confused, and questioning whether I was imagining what just happened.

This makes no sense. Tears are welling up in my eyes. He's my teacher, my mentor, my best friend! I'm sure he didn't mean it in any other way than a friendly gesture. I must be misunderstanding things.

I am lying in my sleeping bag feeling inexplicably guilty. I am trying to erase what is happening but my self-esteem issues are bubbling to the surface causing any normal or rational thought to be impossible.

If rational thought *were* possible, I would realize I have unknowingly given all my power to DJ. If he says jump I'd be the first asking where and how high. I don't get that I am caught in the web, blinded by misplaced loyalty.

There is NO sleep for me tonight. Hour by painful hour I spend in a drenching panic attack.

I watch as the sunrise comes, bringing more and more light to the tent. I try to remain in hiding, pulling my sleeping bag over my head.

Little do I know, things are about to go from bad to worse. The shadow on my soul is out to play.

CHAPTER 5

My mind goes over the cliff

I finally peek my head out from under my sleeping bag, my breath escaping me. I crawl over to the corner of the tent window and look out seeing most of the group is up and about.

I realize there is no more hiding.

All night long I lay awake in anxiety with flashes of fear-driven stories of the past tormenting my mind. I have been dreading this moment. It's become clear that I must go out there and face the awkwardness of the night before.

I throw back the sleeping bag, get up and go to the tent door. Before leaving I take in a long deep breath.

"You can do this, it was nothing." I hone in on the sound of me unzipping the tent. "I made it all up in my head. It was nothing but a friendly gesture."

Thinking these thoughts gives me a momentary sense of relief. I step out onto the dirt turning back briefly to zip up the tent. I am now very aware of my surroundings, sensing everything. *Where is he?* I begin to shiver from head to toe. The chilly fall morning has made an announcement. I pull my hoodie over my head and walk over to the fire.

"Good morning, Beautiful" Artemis greets me with twinkling eyes and a soothing voice, giving a much needed sense of grounding. She catches on to my dismay. "Are you okay?"

I am scanning out of the corner of my eye, trying to locate DJ.

"I'm okay," I say, dishonest as ever.

The truth is I am a complete and utter wreck but unable to tell her. My panic is beginning to rise again, bringing on an extremely nauseous feeling. I know Artemis is catching onto the fact that something's *really* wrong. She comes over and gives me a long hug. "You know I am here for you if you want to talk." Why I don't say anything is beyond me.

As she pulls back, my fractured reality becomes consumed by fear. I can see DJ walking toward us. I want to run and hide. I cannot even talk, swallow, or function. Panic has once again set in.

"Good morning, Jo," he says as he passes by with his voice in my ear like the hiss of a snake. He is creeping me out. My thoughts are racing. What's going on? What has happened? I somehow manage to mutter a "Good morning."

The hustle of the morning is about breaking down camp, packing it up, and heading back to his house. His place is where we usually end class weekends. Everyone has their car there and will soon be departing to go back to the various cities they are from. I have been keeping my distance from DJ, trying to function to the best of my ability, acting like nothing is wrong. The energy between us feels like that of a fighting couple, which I am completely baffled by. In my mind, he is my teacher, a man of wisdom who is twenty-two years my elder.

I wish I could tell you the snapshot of who I am at this moment is different than what it is, but I cannot. I am in a really unfortunate space. As I mentioned, I have no self-esteem. Zippo. It's non-existent. And to further compound the matter I don't even know it. I think my way of being is normal. I have no self-worth. I don't even know what self-worth is. I walk around the world truly believing I don't matter. I have no connection to personal power. I have no concept of what boundaries are or any understanding of being entitled, as a human, to setting them and setting them firmly. I believe I exist in this world to please everyone, even at the cost of myself or what is good (and safe) for me. I believe wholeheartedly that everyone else, especially DJ, knows what is best for me.

I also carry immense heartache from numerous encounters with men who were ultimately less than friendly. With all my heart I am longing to unite with my soulmate, the one I have always known I would meet. I have come to think I am crazy for believing he even exists, but my heart knows differently. I am beyond gullible. To illustrate just how gullible I am, let me share a story with you.

In the recent past, I was taken out on what is called "snipe hunting." It was intended as a joke but I thought it was for real. Some of my country friends thought it would be funny to have some fun with the San Francisco city girl. Snipe hunting is where one takes a paper bag, goes out into nature, slaps on the bag it until a "snipe" comes running into the bag. I was told a snipe is a furry flying bird like rodent animal. I fell for it. Yes, I was out in nature, with an open brown bag, banging on it looking for a snipe. My friends thought my belief was a joke. I wasn't joking.

The icing on the cake is I have no idea life can be any different from the heartache and low self-esteem I live in. To me, there is no other possible way.

I have bought into the false belief that blinds me into believing *this is how it is*. If someone were to ask how I am doing I would say I am rocking it! I have put DJ onto a pedestal, giving him a God-like status. Whatever he says is gold to me. I believe *his way* is the way. I have completely given up my power without even realizing it.

(In five years, on the third day after his death, I will look back and begin to see clearly what is transpiring. For now, I am blinded by my rose colored sunglasses, thinking everyone is of good intention.)

We are still at camp packing up the vehicles, about ready to go back to DJ's. I am holding back tears as I gather my stuff sensing the daggers of energy DJ is sending my way.

"I think you better ride with me," he sneers from behind as he throws stuff into the back of the car. In my panicked state, I battle thoughts between the comfort of his direction and the disgust I feel toward the sudden pull of unwanted intimacy. I am feeling helpless, lost in a sea of sheer overwhelm. It has consumed me.

"I don't feel so well, DJ." I turn to him, facing him for the first time since last night. His piercing blue eyes are locked onto to mine.

"I know, Jo. That's why you need to ride with me."

His familiar supportive tone beckons me to agree. I don't know what else to do. I burst into tears. They are uncontrollable and I am not even sure where they are coming from. He puts his arm around me and takes me to the passenger side door and opens it.

"Get in," he says with an odd persuasive gentleness nobody could refuse, especially given the nature of my internal climate at the moment. Without further question, I get in.

It's not uncommon in our shamanism circle for one of us to be in meltdown and for DJ to be there to help us privately. It's happens every weekend we are together. What was going on with me looked like just another "meltdown" and my classmates supported me from afar, giving me my space.

The car ride back is quiet except for my tears that come and go, yet the tension in the air could be cut with a knife.

"You need to stay and talk to me before you head back to San Francisco." His words break the silence startling me.

Without thinking I nod my head yes. I do not say a word. There is a long and awkward pause.

"I think there is something you're not telling me," he says. He's planting the seed. "Something you want to say but haven't." His words are uncomfortable and confusing the living daylights out of me. Had I not given all my power to him I would have told him firmly to *back off.*

We're back at the Ranch, DJs home, and here I sit on the porch, utterly unable to move other than to get up to give my classmates a halfway hug as they are leaving. I am trying to get myself together enough to drive back to San Francisco.

The last classmate leaves and it's now just me, DJ, and his "roommate" and co-teacher, Nicole, who is inside busy with unpacking from the camping trip. They live together as friends and coworkers. At least that is what we've been told up to this point.

I am sitting on the deck in an old chair. The sun is beaming through the trees glistening on my skin with warmth. The rays of light are twinkling, making it seem as if there are fairies in the air. For a moment I feel relief. Suddenly, DJ comes out the door followed by his two wolf dogs. He pulls up a chair and sits directly in front of me. I lift my head to face him, still feeling fear and panic.

We sit in a piercing silence for a few seconds. "We need to talk." He stares straight into my eyes. His tone is a little less terrifying but I am still feeling very uneasy. He doesn't miss a beat. "You need to think about what it is you're not telling me and let me know." He is leaning forward with his arms on his knees in a posture of presence. There is another awkward silence.

"I don't know DJ … I don't know what you are saying to me."

I am sheepish with my reply, lacking the courage to ask him directly what he is talking about or what last night was all about. I have a tremendous fear of confrontation, especially when it comes to disappointing *him*, so I'm avoiding it at all costs.

"You will need to figure out what you are feeling and tell me, Jody."

There is an uneasy hint of frustration in the tone of his voice. "If you stop panicking you will see clearly what is here." He is being bold and direct. "You've known this between us all along."

That pricked my awareness. I think I am starting to catch on to what he is implying. Is he hinting at what I think he is hinting at?! Oh my God! *He was really trying to hold my hand last night.*

My mind is racing back through the last eight months and all that I have shared with him. There isn't much I haven't told him. He knows my heart, my dreams, and my vulnerabilities. Little do I know, he's taken my truth and used it to build, layer by layer, irrefutable ammunition that will charge this hunt to the point of no return. He has led me to think I am putting "things" together but what is really happening is I am picking up on his trail of bait. There is a peculiar internal shuffling going on inside of my mind. I begin to question everything. "Could it be?" As if he knows where I am, he grabs my hand and gives it a squeeze. It startles me.

"Take the time you need to get yourself together," he says, "and I will walk you out when you are ready to go." He lets go of my hand. "And, I will want to talk to you tonight by phone to make sure you are okay."

With that, he pushes the chair back and heads to the house. The wolf pups stay with me as if they sense I need protection.

Talk to me by phone? That's odd, we never speak by phone. Alone, I sit for another hour in question and prayer. "What is going on, God?" I pray softly.

I hear what I think is only silence.

The car ride back to San Francisco is intense. Three hours of zooming down the freeway with flashing thoughts painting worlds of possibilities. I feel as if my mind has been blown. Could it be? Could it be that my soulmate is showing up differently than I've ever imagined and known? But what about how I felt last night? All the panic? All the ickyness?

But, I trust DJ with my whole heart. He knows what's best for me better than anyone … better than I do. He is my best friend and he's connected to my spirit guides. He must know something that I don't. Maybe there is something I am missing. I trust everything he says. I adore him as my Teacher and I know without a doubt he wouldn't mislead me.

But I am not attracted to him. And he is twenty-two years older than me. What is going on?

The entire three hours home are spent in a flurry of thoughts bouncing back and forth. Yes. No. Yes. No way! Circle after circle they go. My old view of him begins to lose hold. The simplicity of DJ being only my teacher and mentor begins to break down.

By the time I arrive home my heart is strangely opening to him in new ways. There is a bizarre sense of romance. Not a playful, lighthearted romance of two people who truly love one another. It's a romance that is generated out of a darkness of intent that blinds the receiver, me.

In my vulnerable state—post drugs, living in a world of zero self-worth—I take the bait. I've never known love, so this not being it isn't obvious to me.

With a whirlwind of magic I go from resistant panic to greeting the shadow, thinking it is the light.

CHAPTER 6

This is how it begins

Standing outside in the foggy San Francisco air I am fumbling with my keys, trying to unlock my apartment door. I am at my wit's end attempting to regain composure before going in.

I live with my little sister, Dani, who I don't want to worry. I know the events of the weekend are written all over me. I am having little to no luck pulling it together. I unconsciously thrust through my apartment door in a whirlwind of trembling clustered energy.

"Whoa," Dani jumps in her chair. "What the heck happened to you? Are you okay?"

No luck hiding here. Of course she knows something is up. She knows me better than almost anyone and can read me like a book.

"Dani, I am not sure what is happening." I drop my bag at the door bursting at the seams with an odd mixture of sheer terror and awkward excitement. "Do you have a minute to talk?" She can see my eyes are puffy from the last twenty-four hours of on and off tears. My head is spinning with the bait of the weekend going rat-tat-ta-tat in my mind.

"Absolutely I do."

Her face is grimacing with concern. She closes her book and joins me at the front door. She gestures to my bedroom. "Let's go in there." My room is fairly large and cozy, able to give us a little privacy from our other roommate, Francine.

Later, I will recognize this moment, this talk with my little sister, as an extraordinary gift from God. But for now that recognition is not on the horizon for I am lost in the abyss.

We take a seat on my bed. Dani is fully present in her amazingly loving way. I begin to tear up, as I look her straight in the eyes. I confide everything that's gone on with her. Every detail is being confessed. I am sharing about the hand holding disgust, and the panic sleepless night that followed. I am telling her about the conversation at DJ's after class and the way he was hinting at something but I wasn't clear what it was.

"He kept saying I already know. I don't know what he means by that, Dani. It's brought up a lot of questions and thoughts that have raced through my mind the whole way back home. Now they are front and center. I don't know what to do."

I am completely thunderstruck with confusion, thinking *he could be the one*. With every word I say to Dani I begin talking myself into the possibility of him being someone of significance. My heart seems to be opening by way of love, but it's not. What's at play is guilt coming from fear of rejection and abandonment.

"You know I've always known someone in my heart, Dani."

"Yes, I do." She says gently with her beautiful angelic eyes holding me.

"On the way home, after I left his house, I began to think maybe, just maybe, *that* someone is just showing up in a different package, in a different energy."

"Maybe," she says, supporting me unconditionally but yet very hesitant. She has never met DJ. She only knows of him what I have shared with her.

"It would make sense," I continue trying to make this right in my mind, "he and I that is, with all of our similar beliefs in God and spirituality and how we hold honor and integrity close to our hearts." I unknowingly continue to talk myself into the biggest nightmare of my life. The seeds have been planted, the bread crumbs have been laid, and here I am engulfed in a trance of a man I think I can trust with my entire being.

Dani, sensing where I am, places her hand on mine. "Only you can know what's true for you, Jo."

With that, a light bulb goes off! "What's true for me?" I ask myself, connecting to a sacred space inside that holds this knowing so dear.

"I know what is true for me, Dani." I say with an air of excitement. "I always have." I pause in retrospection. "I know what I am going to do."

"What's that?" she says, perking up in response to my inspiration.

"I am going to write DJ a letter and be open and honest about what I've always known."

This feels honorable and aligned. "I will start tomorrow and give it to him next time I see him." This idea seems to make sense and bring me some peace.

Dani and I continue to talk for about another hour. There is an obvious blessing that she is here for me during this peculiar time of vulnerability. Yet, there is the deeper, layered blessing, in that she knows about us, me and DJ, before anything gets started. That she remains my faithful confidant and daily sounding board through it all until the very end (when he dies, six years later) is extraordinary.

DJ has full knowledge of her awareness from the get go. From the very first phone call on the very first night, I told him she knew. He seemed unaffected by it and played it up to be a good thing. On a date soon to come, the one where we agree to keep "us" secret, there is not much he can say about her knowing. She knows ... everything. I thank God for that.

The first phone call with DJ is a doozy. I hear the phone ringing on the nightstand from across the room. Without seeing who it is, I *know* who it is. I walk over and sure enough I see it's DJ's number. My stomach drops. *What do I say? We've never talked on the phone before.*

Butterflies are pounding in my stomach. They are not the normal butterflies of excitement even though they are trying to counterfeit themselves as such. I am caught in the shadow of a fictitious light, seducing me into believing its promise as truth. My body responds.

I answer the phone nervously. "Hello?" I am trying to focus on the familiar sounds of buses and people humming outside my window, but I am having very little luck. All I can hear is my heartbeat and the static on the other end of the phone.

"Hello, Jo." His words strike down anything remotely familiar or secure to me. For an instant part of me desperately wants to hang up the phone. Instead, I respond, "Hello DJ."

And, this is where it begins.

CHAPTER 7

His voice dissolves my world

As I listen to his voice over the phone, the world I once knew is fading away. With every word I find myself further entangled in his web.

There is an awkward playfulness to our conversation. An uncanny air of invisible force continues to support the breakdown of DJ as simply my Teacher. I am blind to any rational thought or reasoning stemming from an unhealed past. The ability to have supportive loving thoughts for myself is out the door.

I have given my power to this man as my Teacher and now he is coming for more.

I am present to an unconscious sense that I had better engage or the consequences will be grim. With my twisted state of emotion and dysfunctional skew on life, I am now fully engaged in the wiring of this being something of a romance.

He wastes no time to pick up on our conversation from earlier in the day.

"Did you have time to think about what I said you to?" I realize he has cut right to the chase. I am silent, searching through my mind for the right thing to say. The cat has got my tongue.

He presses on, "Are you willing to tell me what you have not been willing to tell me, Jo?"

Even though his words and tone try to be kind, there is an indescribable pressure. My thoughts become confused again. I am feeling very vulnerable and his questioning is compounding my state of being. I take a deep breath, close my eyes, and with a leap of faith I throw my heart out there.

"Yes, DJ, I have thought a lot about what you said. The whole way home, actually."

My heart is pounding in my chest like a loud native drum. I feel raw and tender from the emotions of the last twenty-four hours. All the sideways reflection has thrown me off. It is so odd to be opening up to him in this way. Without knowing why, I continue to push through my awkwardness.

"I've thought a lot about you and me."

My breath is shallow and my voice slightly trembling. "I even had a really long conversation with my little sister about it when I got home. You know how close we are."

My chest is tight. I am feeling resistant to saying anything further. Part of me wants to end the conversation immediately. Do I say it? I attempt to summon up the courage to tell him I think I may be feeling romantic feelings toward him. But do I really? I feel so much pressure. How odd is this?

As if on cue, he meets my worries head on.

"You know you can tell me anything," he says, "I will not judge you. I am the closest person to you, Jo." He is beckoning forth an agreement, one that can only come from the soul living in my body. He continues, "You know I love you unconditionally."

With that, he succeeds, and the floodgates begin to open. With another deep breath I begin to share the nature of the last five hours on the car ride home and the in-depth conversation I had with my little sister.

"Yes, DJ, I know I can trust you with anything," I begin surrendering. There are a few seconds of dead air that feels like an eternity. It has become clear that not saying anything is no longer an option. *Here I go!* I think. *I am jumping off a cliff and giving away my heart.*

"DJ, all I know is I need to be honest with you. It goes against my own integrity not to. Last night when you held my hand by the fire it felt weird and it felt scary."

He doesn't miss a beat. "I could tell. Why did that freak you out so much?" His voice is intentional and focused as if he is navigating where I am going.

"Well, it felt like it was more than a friendly gesture." My heart is now beating in my throat as the walls between us begin to break down. I feel completely exposed and he knows it. It's exactly where he wants me to be. No more hiding. I continue on, "You're always affectionate with us. But that felt different and it freaks me out."

"What about it freaks you out?"

I take a moment to pause. "Well, you're my Spiritual Teacher, DJ, and it freaks me out because it felt, well, it felt very uncomfortable. Very different than I imagined my Spiritual Teacher would be with me. It felt intimate and I didn't like it."

There is another awkward pause as I am teetering on the fence between friend and foe.

"It *is* different Jo." His voice is now serious and gripping. "Things between me and you are different than they are with the other students. We are meant for something different." The seed is subtly being planted deeper as he is catching onto my resistance. "And, if it was more than a friendly gesture toward you, then what?"

My emotions are whirling. I throw up a small wall: "You're my spiritual Teacher, DJ."

"Yes, I am, so when I say there is something different between us you must trust me on that." The past eight months of figuring out what makes me tick, of honing in on the world of my heart and building up irrefutable trust are beginning to pay off for him. With a final plunge into the unknown I jump again.

"I'm not sure what I am feeling DJ. There is a part that wonders if you are more to me than just my teacher. I am wondering if I am feeling romantic feelings toward you." I can sense the huge relief on the other end of the phone.

"Jo, I already know the answer to that one."

I deflect his comment. The fear has come back full force. I burst out the only thing I know to say to him. "I need some time to sort out how I feel."

CHAPTER 8

A shadow of betrayal descends

Flash forward through a time warp to the second day after I got the news of DJ's death. I call it Day Two of doomsday unraveling.

It's four in the morning, and with a gasp of air I sit up in bed.

"Stay away from me!" I am swinging my fists fiercely through the air flinging them at something that's not there. I realize I am dreaming and begin to cry. Wade rolls over and puts his hand softly on my back.

"It's going to be okay, Jody."

I am so thankful the dysfunction of our relationship has been put on the back burner for now. Fighting one of our gruesome fights at this time would have killed me.

"Are you going to be okay?" It time for Wade to go train one of his early morning clients. I nod my head yes. He moves his hand from my back and goes to get out of bed. "I will be back in a couple of hours." He changed his schedule a bit so he can be here for me. I think he may be a little worried about how I am doing.

I throw the covers over my head and try to go back to sleep. The morning does not stop however. It keeps rolling on, as I stay tucked under the covers wishing to be like an ostrich. I really want to stick my head in the ground, pray for this all to be over, and have someone come get me when it is done. The Canadian geese outside my window are in their morning ritual of welcoming in the sun. As I listen to their deep echoing honks I think of how this sound, once welcomed, is now a reminder of something awful.

I feel achingly alone in my thoughts. I'm aware of a heavy burden on my soul. *Do I say anything, God?* Tears roll down my face as I desperately cling for some clarity. *I gave my word.* And nobody has asked. That was the deal. That was my word. I must honor that.

I am in an internal battle. I am being pulled and stretched to the limits of what I can handle. The secret of the shadow on my soul has become a heavy load, forcefully taking its toll on me. "Where are you, God?" I say out loud in prayer. "I need you."

I am only able to hear silence all around me, but God is with me.

"I've got to get up. I can't lie here alone anymore."

I toss the covers back and somehow manage to pull myself out of bed and head downstairs. I am dragging my anxiety with me like a bag of forbidden treasure. It's been more than a couple of hours since Wade has gone to train his client and now I see he is back, sitting in his favorite chair in our living room. I am happy to see him home. I don't want to be alone.

I have stopped eating and I am hardly drinking water. Not by choice. My body has shut down. My mouth is parched with dryness from the roller coaster of emotions and anxiety. I have yet to hear from Nicole, who is now my business partner, and DJ's wife. My heart is aching for her. In the past couple of years they had taken their twenty-year friendship into a romantic partnership.

My mind races in thought. *I can only imagine how hard this is on her to lose him.* I have grown to love Nicole and even though there is an unspoken tension between us, I know in my heart we can sort that out.

We have recently opened a healing arts studio together in downtown Nevada City, California. Our grand opening is scheduled for next Friday. I will be leaving my day job to fully dedicate time to our studio. It's a dream come true. I know there will be ample space and time for us to have a heart-to-heart. It's becoming clear to me I need to do so for the sake of my own integrity.

I sigh. My heart is heavy in anticipation of our conversation. The shadow on my soul is blinding, and the only way I believe I can see again is to talk to Nicole.

I join Wade in our living room. The sun is shining through the windows with a golden shimmer of light, giving me a momentary sense of comfort. I am thankful it's not the dead of winter when this is going on. Something about it being spring lightens the load a tad.

Our living room is a beautiful space. We have floor-to-ceiling windows that look out over the lake. Wade and I are enjoying small talk when our house phone begins to ring. The piercing sound causes me to flinch. I am looking over at the phone with disgust, as if it is personally assaulting me. The second ring comes through. My stomach drops to the floor as I become nauseous. I know who it is. I slowly swallow and try to regain composure. *Why do I feel so sick?*

As I listen to Wade answer the phone, negative energy begins to race through to the core of my being. I begin to panic, though I'm not quite sure why.

"It's for you," Wade says handing me the phone. "It's Nicole."

My stomach drops again to the floor and all I can feel is my worried heart racing. *What is my problem?* Time has become liquid quicksand, dragging me face to face to years of heaviness and darkness I have been unconsciously carrying around. I take the phone from Wade in what feels like slow motion. His eyes are halfway perturbed yet supportive. I walk into our spare bedroom and close the door.

"Hi Nicole," I manage to mutter. "How are you doing?"

I feel strange asking such a thing since I know damn well how she is doing. There is a piercing silence on the other end of the phone.

"Jody," she says, dismissing my question, "I have to ask you something and I want you to be very honest with me."

"Of course I will, Nicole." At this point I feel as if I am dreaming a really bad dream, yet not knowing why or how. I am hanging on every word she says while holding on to every space between her words. "What is it?" I feel poked and prodded by demons.

The deafening silence continues.

"Please just ask me," I say with a jolt that gives the conversation momentum

"Jody, I don't know how to ask this other than to be direct"

I do not like her tone.

"Be direct, I will not lie to you."

My world is shifting and spinning around me. I literally feel dizzy. The years of the unspoken is coming to the light. The "pause" button of the past is about to release into full forward momentum.

"Jody," she says, "Were you and my husband ever intimate?"

The bomb has dropped! THANK GOODNESS SOMEONE FINALLY HAS ASKED. My entire world comes to a thundering halt, a climax of shadow meeting light. I burst into tears. Years of pent-up energy begin to pour forth, lifting from my stifled soul.

"Thank God you asked me, Nicole." The tears pour from my eyes. I have been waiting for this moment for a long time.

"Thank God someone has finally asked me."

I am sobbing uncontrollably with a strange sense of relief. Like a weight has been lifted off of me.

"YES, Nicole, yes, we were intimate. He was my boyfriend and we were lovers for two and a half years. We got together when I first started studying with him. I wanted to tell you from the beginning and for some reason DJ didn't want to do that. I knew you would understand since it was before you guys were ever together."

The floodgates have opened and there is no stopping the flow of truth coming from my lips. I continue with a pleading of spirit.

"He asked that I never tell anyone about us. I never understood why he didn't want to tell anyone, but I agreed to keep it between us out of honor to him. He was adamant about not telling you, but I told him if anyone asked I'm not going to lie! It goes against my integrity. You are the first person to ask, Nicole. I am so sorry for never telling you!"

My heart is wrenching with bittersweet release. I am crying out, begging God to have her understand. But I am deaf to what is going on the other end. I finally take a breath long enough to hear her sobbing.

That's to be expected. I am not prepared for what I hear next.

"Oh no Jody! No, no, no! He did it to you too." She is firing at me with a vengeance. "Did he tell you that? Did he tell you we were never intimate or together before a couple of years ago?"

"Yes, Nicole he did. He said you guys got married out of convenience from a promise he made to your dying dad that he would marry you in order for you to be legal here in the US. Is that not true?"

My stomach drops, my chest tightens, feeling as if my body does not exist any longer. I feel as if I am literally dying. Flashes of times spent with DJ are popping up in my mind like images on a screen. Pieces of a jigsaw puzzle are beginning to be put together. Subtle things I couldn't put my finger on are now becoming clear. The more Nicole discloses, the more light is shed on the shadow on my soul. I am bewildered by her words. *How can this be? What is she saying to me?!*

"Oh my God, he did it to you too!" Her tone is stabbing with utter disgust and disappointment. *Did what?* I am thinking in an almost defensive way. *What is she talking about? He wouldn't do anything to me. He loved me.*

"Jody, DJ and I have been together and having sex for over twenty years. We have spent countless hours making love. We've *never* been just friends. He has been my husband the whole time. How could you do this?!"

What she is saying is beginning to sink in as I freak out. "Oh my God … I was a *mistress* and didn't even know it?!! How could he do this?!! How could this be happening?!" I want to crawl out of my skin, into a hole, and die. "Help me God."

SLAMMMMM!!!! The first cracking swing of the spiritual sledgehammer has awakened my soul. I am in a state of shock beyond any I thought possible, unable to process the realization that the man I adored and loved with all my heart and soul is a liar, a fake, and a betrayer.

One would think this day would be enough to fill the tall order of "God never gives us more than we can handle," but for me, this is not the end. This is the beginning of yet another layer to the unfolding.

What happens on the next day will forever define strength of heart.

CHAPTER 9

And the news gets harder to hear

I am in a messy and chaotic tumble of words with Nicole. I am utterly stunned, sitting on the edge of the bed in our spare bedroom completely speechless.

How can this be?!

Even though I hear sounds coming from her mouth I am completely beside myself, unable to retain what she is saying. She is panicked and rambling on now about how he has destroyed her. In and out of reality I go.

"Do I come to the funeral?" I say to her.

I answer before she can: "No, I can't come to the funeral. I have no idea who DJ is or was. I can't face you and everyone. I am such a horrible person."

I am now internalizing full blame for what has happened. I should have known ... how did I not know? I'm sinking into utter disgust with myself. All the smooth sailing confidence I was feeling for my life and myself a few days ago, before his death, has just sailed into a brick wall.

I hang up the phone without saying goodbye. I drop the phone on the bed, walk to the bedroom door sobbing. I open it feeling like I am walking through a nightmare.

Wade is sitting patiently in silence in his chair.

I make a beeline for him. Without saying a word I sit down right in front of him, my head hanging low. I grab his hands with tears streaming down my face. I am so ashamed I cannot even look up. It would take all my courage and energy to raise my head right now and look him straight in the eyes. Instead I keep my head down. "I'm a horrible person, Wade." He squeezes my hand. By the grace of God I muster up enough inner strength to look up.

"There is something I have been wanting to tell you."

He is sitting quietly as he waits for the download. I am trying to catch my breath and quiet the tears long enough to say what I have wanted to say for years.

"It's DJ, Wade."

I am freaking out inside, not sure how to tell him the deep, dark, icky secret I've been hiding all this time.

Finally I blurt it out, "DJ and I were together romantically for two and a half years. When I first started studying with him he became my boyfriend. I wanted to tell you, but he made me promise to keep it a secret from everyone. And I agreed."

The sobbing has come back as I am consumed with flashes of my conversation with Nicole and the realization that DJ was not who I thought he was; nor was my relationship with him what I thought it was. I am gasping for air. I somehow keep talking.

"But I told him if anyone ever asked I would tell them. *No one* asked. Not you. Not my family. Now, finally someone has asked. It was Nicole! She just asked me right now!"

I am trying to process what is going on. A wave of despair comes over me. Everything is melting. I still go on.

"And, what's the worst part is Nicole just told me *they* were intimate and having sex for over twenty years!"

I feel sick inside of my skin thinking of all the times DJ had touched my body, made love to me, and then went home to his secret wife and did who knows what. I place my head into my hands.

I keep talking to Wade, "That means I was a mistress and didn't even know it!" Wade squeezes my hand in a gesture to pull me back to reality. "I am a horrible human being!" I now fully hate myself.

"Jody," Wade's voice sounds like that of an angel. "Don't say that."

For all the fighting we have done in the recent past, his suddenly showing up in this time of pain is a Godsend. I look up at him wiping my nose on my sleeve like a little girl. I try to look away. I feel so much shame.

"Look at me, Jody."

I turn my head to face him not sure if I will make it to my next breath.

"Hear me when I say this to you." He is looking me directly in the eyes with his hands firmly holding mine. "Can you hear me?"

I nod my head yes. The words he says next blow my concept of reality into tiny little pieces.

"You are not the only one!"

Like a knife, his words stab me.

"What?!" I sit on the couch, stunned with confusion. "What do you mean I'm not the only one? What does that mean?"

I think he is talking nonsense yet he has my full attention. He continues, "I met DJ here at my birthday party a few months back, remember?" Wade now has a sarcastic tone intended to catch my attention.

"Yes, I remember."

"I shook his hand, and when I did I immediately *knew* he was a predator."

"Predator?!" I exclaim, feeling threatened by such a comment. I am trying to grasp what he is saying to me.

"No!" I protest, "That's not possible! He would never do that!" But as I am speaking there is a part of me beginning to realize there may be truth to what he is saying.

"I promise you, Jody, you will receive a phone call soon and you will find out you are not the only one. I know predators."

Boy, as I will soon see, he is (so unfortunately) right about this.

Tomorrow on day three after the news of DJ's death, the spiritual sledgehammer takes a third and final swing, knocking me to my knees, eliminating anything and everything I know as truth.

CHAPTER 10

The calm before a new storm

Day Three of the doomsday unraveling:
It's another night of little to no sleep. Frustrated, I open my eyes and throw the covers back to get out of bed. I lay for a moment noticing my skin is damp from waves of anxiety throughout the night. I roll over and realize Wade has gone to work. My stomach drops. I hate being alone right now.

I get up to stumble to the bathroom where I place my hands on the counter to catch myself. I raise my head, looking straight into my own eyes in the mirror.

I can do this. I can face this day.

This living nightmare is taking its toll on me. All I want to do is crawl back into bed and go back to sleep. Permanently. Instead, I am left to my own plaguing thoughts: *Could it be true? Could it possibly be true that DJ would do that?* With that thought, once again, tears begin to stream down my face.

I continue to try to grapple with reality, praying for this to all be a really bad dream. The stinging tears on my cheek and dark puffiness of the bags under my eyes tell me this is very real. Shock is a peculiar thing. Here I stand, alone in our beautiful bathroom, looking into the mirror, only able to see a dark unknown creature being reflected back to me.

I have no idea who you are.

I am filled with a self-hatred, hatred I would not wish on my worst enemy. I see no other option but to blame myself. I continue to stare at my image in the mirror trying to find the old me. Staring back is a face that looks as if it has been through a war. I have no idea who this is looking at me.

Somebody make it stop … I am pleading under my breath in a whisper in the hopes an angel may hear me. I hear nothing but a deafening silence. My heart sinks even further. *That's right, God doesn't love me either. He has left me.* This is the furthest thing from the truth but I cannot see that yet.

How could this be happening? DJ and I were in love! We were supposedly soulmates!

I feel myself trying to reach for something to grasp to make sense of this. *He said* we were soulmates! He said he loved me like he never loved another. He even showed me how our astrological charts were the same! Oh, what a fool I am.

I stumble a few more steps to the toilet and grab some tissue to blow my nose. My movements seem orchestrated by something outside myself. I feel very little conscious connection to my body. The world around me is wobbly and foggy. I walk back to the mirror and pause. I take a breath and look into my eyes once again in hopes that maybe the dark creature has gone away. No luck. The demon still stares back. I lose my breath placing my face back into my hands. The tears of heartache and betrayal continue to stain my soul. I have no forgiveness for myself for what has happened.

How come I didn't feel anything when he died?! Why would he do this? I trusted him wholeheartedly!

I am in an internal boxing match, seeing no other option than to beat myself up for what has transpired.

I have been keeping my distance from yesterday's conversation with Wade, the one where he suggested I was one of many. There is no room in my psyche for that idea. I am in a state of shock and any more information will throw me over the edge.

But the truth of his words is starting to percolate.

I have always considered myself to be a strong woman, a woman of very few tears. (At least tears that others could see.) I pride myself on never being a victim. Right now, I am trying to hold true to that, but I am a mess and there is no controlling it. My negative thoughts return with a vengeance:

I felt my Grandma, my dear friend Jerico, and others who have died. I knew the exact moment when they left. I felt them come to me to say goodbye. How come, God, how come I did not know that DJ, my supposed soulmate, died!?

My thoughts lean into Nicole and their relationship.

And, how could he sleep with me and then sleep with her at the same time and LIE TO ME!

With that, I barely make it back to the bed where I collapse myself into a crying slumber.

Soon enough I awaken to the presence of Wade's hand on my back. With a gasp of air I open my eyes, roll over, and see him standing above me. I feel disoriented and confused.

"Are you alright, Jody?" He is reaching for my hand.

I take his hand as he gently pulls me up and out of bed and into his arms. I am so thankful for his kindness the last few days. It has been a Godsend.

"Have you eaten anything today Jody?" His concerned tone flashes me back to the dark creature I saw staring at me in the mirror earlier today.

"I look like shit, don't I?" I pull back from his embrace trying not to connect with his eyes.

He doesn't let go. "No, you don't look like shit, but it's been a rough couple of days. Go easy on yourself."

His hand caresses my cheek in a way I haven't felt since the very first week we met each other. His touch is free of animosity or anger. He gestures to the bedroom door. "Let's go downstairs and get you something to eat." I feel so relieved and take him up on his offer.

It's not long before I am in the kitchen staring out the window, lost in thought. The sun is beaming with a glimmering shimmer on top of the water, lending a momentary sense of peace. Wade, who is busy cooking up a little something for breakfast on the stovetop, takes no notice. There is a slight breeze cascading beautiful sunlight patterns, making ripples that are mesmerizing and soothing to my soul.

We have two Canadian geese that have adopted us and our home. We've watched as they birthed their families here for the last two years. We've named them Fred and Ethel. I watch as they walk their babies across our yard and for a moment I am envious, wishing nothing more than to be out of the hell I am now in. My daydream doesn't last long. Like a flash, I snap back into my body and there it is, front and center, my broken heart.

"What are you thinking?" Wade is handing me a plate of something that looks similar to eggs, potatoes, and toast. (He was never much of a cook.)

"I am thinking this is all a really bad dream."

I walk over to the table, sit down and attempt to eat, but it does not taste very good. I sigh, put the fork down, and once again my face goes into my hands. My eyes are beginning to sting from the tears. I am trying with all my might to hold them back. I look up, turning to Wade who has taken a seat next to me.

I say to him, "I've been thinking about what you said. About me not being the only one. I don't know if I believe that."

"It doesn't matter if you believe it!!"

Wade's tone is snide. It's leaning a little too much in the

direction of a possible fight. He catches himself and regains his composure.

"I'm telling you, Jody. He is a predator."

All of a sudden Wade's energy is becoming intense again. His eyes are widening, looking as if he may blow a circuit. I am beginning to get nervous. I know the signs of his aggression. He literally growls at me, "I tell you, if he were not dead I would let him know in a way he could not forget how angry I am that he ever hurt you! I cannot stand that he took advantage of you!"

His anger is rising. He has always had a really hard time with the idea that anyone would hurt me. His protective nature goes way beyond normal, often times scaring me. It has always confused me. I have no idea where it comes from.

"I know, Wade. I know it really bothers you."

"Do you, Jody? Then why would you have gotten yourself in this situation?!"

I knew his kindness couldn't last. The tears burst from my eyes.

"I didn't *know*!"

Wade catches himself and grabs my hand. "I'm sorry. That was not a very nice thing for me to say."

I am surprised by his apology.

"It's okay, Wade. I am sure this is rough for you."

Like clockwork, I am back in my codependent people-pleasing mode. I shut down. All I want is peace between us.

That's not going to happen.

With impeccable timing, like something out of a movie, the phone begins ringing. It is piercing. I jump a bit, gasping for air.

CHAPTER 11

Arrival at rock bottom

The sound of the phone is like a knife piercing my soul. My stomach drops. Somewhere beyond physical reality I know what is coming.

Wade gets up from the table and begins to walk over to the phone, "Let me answer it." He takes the lead knowing where I am at emotionally.

It rings again. Piercing. I watch as he picks it up.

I look away, not wanting to be here. In a muffled background I hear what sounds like a gruff exchange. Wades waves for my attention.

"It's for you," he says, reluctantly, "It's Nicole."

I suddenly feel even more nauseous. In slow motion I walk over and take the white cordless phone from Wade's hand. He does not look happy.

"Hi, Nicole." She's frantically sobbing and mumbling something. I am in no way prepared for what is about to come through on the other end.

"Jody! I can't believe it!" She is gasping for air, crying unlike I have ever heard another cry.

"What is it, Nicole?" I am beginning to panic. Wade is standing guard next to me.

"It's horrible, Jody! So horrible!"

"It's okay, Nicole. Take a breath and slow down. Tell me what's going on."

"I opened DJ's safe ... " Her sobbing becomes a wail. "I can't believe it! I thought he loved me!" There is a moment of awkward silence. Then she continues.

"There are countless others!" she blurts out with disgust.

"Countless other what?" Even though I ask the question in the background I am thinking, *Oh my God, was Wade right?*

"Countless other women!" She bursts out into uncontrollable tears. "At least thirty others!" I am in disbelief as I listen to her speak. Despair comes over me, swallowing any last hope DJ was any of what he portrayed himself to be.

"Oh my God, Nicole?! What are you talking about?"

"I found it all! I found all the papers, emails, photos, journals ... I found everything!" I am becoming mortified, flashing back to the countless intimate sexual emails I had sent DJ when we were together. No, I think to myself, he said for us to get rid of those years ago as a closure to our relationship. We had agreed to destroy them in honor of letting go.

"He was sick, Jody. He has pornographic pictures with your head cut out and pasted on them. There's a journal logging everything he had said to you and every other woman! As if he was trying to keep track. This is so wrong! He was my husband!"

With every sobbing sentence she says, the world as I know it becomes destroyed. Rock bottom is quickly approaching.

"And, you, Jody ..." Her tone is piercing, "How could you?"

She begins reading my own words to me from years ago. Words I had intended only for DJ, words that expressed my love and willingness for sexual intimacy. Something I had never done due to a sexually abusive past. As she continues to read I feel as if I am dying before leaving my body. My eyes are wide open but what I have held as the light of God becomes blacked out, frozen, paralyzing me from the inside out.

"I am unable to talk to you anymore, Nicole. This is not alright."

Without another word I hand the phone to Wade and fall to my knees. I curl up into a ball of a sobbing mess. "What is going on God? I thought you were with me?"

I have often heard the term "rock bottom." I have now arrived. In this moment as I am kissing the floor praying for understanding, I now get what that term means.

The only good news is from here on there is only one way to go, and that is up.

However, my visit to rock bottom isn't brief. There are moments to come that will stretch and challenge me in ways that are not for the faint of heart.

But what I will come to see, someday when I am looking back, is I am amidst a blessing. By way of this painful experience I am to eventually be liberated from the false imprisonment I have built around myself. A spiritual two-by-four has knocked me upside the head in service to waking me up. Yes, in this moment, at rock bottom, it hurts. But the blessing is that what is not authentic in me is being chipped away so that I AM can finally be free.

Later the lesson in this will become clear. Life is *always* for us. Even in times like this when it seems it could not possibly be so.

CHAPTER 12

Now it's time to wake up

Even as challenging as these times are, if I could be a butterfly on the wall looking back from my future I would see I am being groomed for a miraculous and beautiful life.

My current circumstances have put me on a bewildering path. I believe I am doomed to living at rock bottom. I may feel as if I am sentenced to this hell with the weight of the world living on my shoulders, but the lovely butterfly from the future knows of something quite different.

It visits from far beyond the *now* knowing wholeheartedly what currently transpires is the gateway to freedom. So, in this light, none of what has happened is bad or wrong. It's now about taking steps to unlock the invisible door so I may walk through. And, as you will see, the key is all about love. Not the giving or receiving of the love of another. Even as wonderful as that is as a pivotal part of the human journey, it's not the love I'm referring to.

The love I am referring is the love of Self. Sounds simple, hippy, or maybe even a little too New Age, but it is absolute truth, **if we do not go within we go without.**

This realm of Self-love I speak of does not navigate through a narcissistic world. That is completely ego. This love of Self I refer to comes from the soul. Loving in this manner is the key to our divine purpose (including sharing this love with another.)

Going inward is not an easy task for most. Especially me!

Here I am lying on the floor in utter despair thinking this is my cursed lot in life! But my current state of reality stems from an unconscious inability to tap into the wealth of my being. Simply put, I can't see yet that I am worthy of love and being loved. I do not have the capacity to yet recognize that our worth is inherent in our humanity. There is no way of NOT being worthy. Just like there is no way to be anything other than Love. Both are inherent in our true nature.

Going inside is every human being's purpose and we all eventually get there. And it is now my turn at bat. I have spent my life deafened and blinded by my own negative judgments, codependency, and lack of self-esteem. But what has happened in the last three days has served as a HUGE wake-up call. I am now wide-eyed and out of my slumber. I have nowhere else to go but within. Everything outside of myself that I once held close has crumbled. I have even shut down from God (even though God has not shut down from me) for the first time in my life. Here I am, feeling alone, scared by the many shades and colors of humanness.

In order to wake up, in order to restore loyalty to my soul, liberation from the seduction of DJ's counterfeit energy had to transpire. The false promise had to be brought to the light. That is what is happening.

I would love to say it is all grace and ease from here, but that is not the case. Grace? Yes. Ease ... well, that's coming. For now, it's all about taking my hand off the snooze button and continuing to wake up.

CHAPTER 13

From one web into another

The little peace Wade and I experienced during the three days after DJs death came to a screeching halt and is now completely gone.

I face each day with a heavy heart, feeling an ever-growing need to protect myself from his laser beam aggression. I am beginning to wonder if I am going insane from the tremendous guilt I carry. These times are not easy, nor are they easy to speak of. Dark shadows of repressed hurt are beginning to come out of me in unbecoming ways that I'm not proud of. Claiming the victim card is not my forté. In fact, my cup of tea is quite the opposite. But I am having a really hard time holding it together.

The little backbone of self-worth and respect I built up for myself by way of my studies and relationship with DJ have been squashed to nothing. I say "self-worth and respect" but in fact they were neither of those, really. The counterfeit energy spanned across the board.

Here I am, filled with repressed hurt, guilt, and unconscious anger, engaged to a man who is not only consumed with rage but who has no problem expressing it outwardly. Not a good combo. It's not pretty.

It's 5:00 a.m. I am half-awake, driving on the winding roads of Grass Valley in the pitch black, heading to the gym.

In this early morning hour the only company I find is a shimmer from the moon. I am fighting back the urge to fall asleep. I am so tired from another fight-filled evening. My saving grace is the upbeat music quietly thumping through the car. I am lost in the reflection of a dead-end dream, confused about what I am doing. Not only am I carrying a heavy load from the emotional trauma of the past couple years, I am also feeling hung over from another night of heavy drinking with Wade.

I am not sure how alcohol has become such a huge part of our relationship. Yet, it has. Every night features more beer and vodka, which usually leads to brutal fighting.

I don't allow myself to see that there is no real hope for this relationship. I am living in a sea of red flags, holding on for dear life to an ideal that cannot be created with him. There is no capacity within Wade's consciousness to create the loving relationship I know in my heart. He is not the one I have known from my dreams. Like DJ, Wade has portrayed himself to be something he is not.

I guess there is truth in the saying, *It takes one to know one.* I am beginning to see that maybe, just maybe, all the violence Wade's ex-wives speak of is not fictitious. The alcohol brings out the demons within him and I respond defensively. I am sucked in. I am feeling alcohol is the only way I can cope with all that is going on. Little do I know, my own addictive nature is extremely codependent, believing the world of Wade's dysfunction. (It is only later that I will be set free from this patterning.)

Right now, I have no skills to process my current reality. I have placed myself in total isolation from those I love. I won't talk to my family even though they continuously reach out to me. Not because I don't want to talk to them. I miss them with all my heart. It stems from fear. There is unspoken hostility from Wade about my family taking up too much of my attention.

I can't see it yet, but my being in total isolation is part of Wade's method of operation to keep me exactly where he wants me, in the web of his control. My circle of friends are gone. Everyone I was close to was a part of DJ's shamanism community. The day he died, out of severe shame, I cut all ties with everyone except Artemis, and even that is hanging by a silk thread. We talked for the first month or two after his death, but now there is little to no communication between us.

I am by no means an innocent victim. The things that are coming out of me these days are not pretty. Even though I think my behavior can be justified as self-defense, I could honor myself by leaving him. I know our being together is mutually unhealthy and dangerous. Maybe some part of me feels I need to be punished for what has happened.

There is no love between us. How could there be? If I do not love myself authentically then I cannot love another. It's the law, just like gravity. If I walk to a cliff and jump, gravity will become very apparent. Trying to love another and be loved by another without loving myself is like walking to a cliff and jumping, thinking I will fly. It's not going to happen. What is within is without. If I do not go within (and heal) I go without. If I loved myself in the first place I would have never attracted a man such as Wade.

I have arrived at the gym.

Wade, being a professional trainer and retired pro body builder, trains my friend Kona and me every morning. I open the car door noticing I feel especially out of sorts today. I groggily walk in the darkness of the morning toward the gym door. I fling it open, foggy in the head, feeling a little anxious as I remember last night's fight. The usual crazy crack ass early morning crew greets me as I walk through the door.

"Good Morning, Jody," I hear from behind the counter.

I lift my head in an attempt to act like nothing is wrong. "Good Morning, Mike."

The morning ritual begins. Mike is another trainer here at the gym who also works the front desk. He has become quite a good friend to us. He is kind and genuine in heart and his cheerfulness is always a spirit-lifter for me. I spot Kona and Wade across the room and begin to walk over to meet them. My stomach begins to tighten at the sight of Wade as I reflect on the horrific words spoken to one another from the night before. I once again try to put on a good face.

I say, "Hi babe." It's all I can manage to mutter to him in an attempt to keep things at a low roar. I am holding my head low feeling as if I could cry.

"Hi," he says and grabs my hand, giving it a slight squeeze with a quick release. I think this is his attempt at apologizing. He looks at me and Kona: "Let's get started, you two!"

He's not an affectionate man. Quite the opposite, actually, which poses a continuous problem for us. My primary language of love is touch. His is not.

He gestures for us to head toward the hack squat to get our workout underway. Kona, an angel of a friend, knows damn well what is going on between us even though I have never mentioned anything to her. Our friendship is unique in that there is an intuitive understanding and communication between us.

We begin our workout per usual. Given we are both very strong, we are lifting some pretty heavy weights with ease. Wade likes to show us off. He likes to make our strength known. I don't particularly care to be the center of attention, especially given I have gained fifty-three pounds. This weight gain is a first in my life, and I can't help but think it's out of protection. Wade's anger scares me.

I don't usually say anything about the discomfort of being a spectacle. Today, however, it's different. I am not feeling well and I must say something.

"Wade, I think this weight is too much."

"No, you can do this ... no problem," he growls. His vocal chords were severed from an accident prior to us meeting, so when he talks it's in a raspy monotone that sounds very much like a growl.

"Jody, don't embarrass me." His monotone rasp has a threatening quality to it. Fear wins and I begin my set on the hack squat, which is a machine used to work the quadriceps. With each rep I feel growing pressure in my head but I push through, not wanting to upset or disappoint Wade. I really believe that I don't matter.

"Wade, I don't feel good." I am at rep three in the first set of twenty reps.

"You can't stop, Jody."

I am feeling pressured to continue and do so against my own inner knowing that there's something going on in my body. All of a sudden, like a flash of lightening, a shooting pain explodes in my head sending a piercing pain that feels like it could deafen me. I am forced to a halt. I grab my head and begin to cry.

Kona grabs my arm, "Oh my God, are you okay?"

Crying is not a usual thing for me. I do my best to hide tears at all cost. Not a healthy choice. Today, however, there is no choice.

"I'm okay," I lied. I walk over to sit down on a nearby chair.

Wade's response is, "Don't overreact, Jody." There is almost disgust in his voice. "I can't believe you." His words are a hiss and his eyes are glaring at me with a rage. I know there will be hell to pay later.

With that he motions to Kona, "Let's go over here. Jody will join us when she wants."

Kona seems confused about what to do.

"I'm fine Kona," I say, "I'll be over in a bit."

I am fighting the tears back as she reluctantly joins him. We are all trying to keep the peace. We know his temper.

Here I am, sitting alone in the gym with excruciating pain in my head stemming from what I think is a pulled neck muscle, while my supposed soon-to-be-husband is over there oblivious to me. Seeing the daunting truth that this man, who supposedly loves me, has harshly rejected and dismissed my wellbeing stuns me. For all we know, this pain could be something serious.

Right now, I no longer feel any sense of safety in my world. The tiny thread of security that was present in my life has left the building. With all my might I try to hide my tears, which are now infused with sadness. I try to focus on my breath and my racing thoughts cause it to escape from me.

I'm thinking, "I've got to get it together enough to head home. I can't do this anymore. I am not going to work today and I don't even care."

Usually I would force myself to go in to work no matter how I feel, but not today. Mike, the other trainer, comes over to check on me.

"Are you okay?" His genuine concern comforts me. I look up at him with thankful eyes.

"I can't do this." I need not explain. He has witnessed the brutality between us.

"What can I do to help you, Jody?" He is an angel to me at the moment.

"Please just let Wade know I went home."

This is a huge moment for me. In the past, I would never

just leave without saying something to him myself. It would always be my codependent habit of sheepishly going over to him, making sure it was okay with him.

But today marks the beginning of the end of that. And, this is a good thing. I am beginning the journey of reclaiming my power.

The entire car ride home is a blur behind tears. Distracted by the physical pain, I, without knowing it, make a plea. "Please God help me." I didn't think it was possible, but my heart has crumbled even more. Lost in my thoughts, I hear a silent beckoning from within asking for a willingness to come out of the sea of red flags. Small and still, I sense the voice inviting the realization that Wade has no capacity to love in the way it is intended for me to love.

I am wallowing around, trying to familiarize myself with rock bottom as if I am going to make it my new home. But, fortunately, that is not the Divine plan. Nor, was it ever intended to be. There is only one way I am heading now, and that is up.

Unbeknownst to me, I am being guided through this. My visit to rock bottom has not been a short one but I am mistaken to think it is a permanent one.

Like flashes on a movie screen, I am remembering moments of fights Wade and I have had recently. With each pang, his rage has magnified into nasty emotional abuse with words so unkind I might rather the abuse be physical. That, too, is lurking in the air. There have been a couple of rude physical pushes so far, from behind, with one that flung me through the air to land on my knees causing bleeding and bruising. He has become vengeful and jealous of a man who is dead, yelling at me on countless occasions such things as "Fuck you! Why don't you go suck that dead man's cock!!"

His words are like cement, seeming to turn the shame and

guilt I feel about DJ into concrete. I know that how I feel and how I respond is completely my business, yet today I am at my wit's end. As I drive back home, on the windy mountain roads, I miss my relationship with God for the first time in a long time. The conscious daily communion I once had with Spirit has been put into the brackets of my stillness awaiting the hope of acceptance and forgiveness. It has been nearly two years since DJ died and nearly two years since I have prayed or talked to God or my angels. It used to be a communication that was as natural as you and me talking.

But, by the grace of love, today all that is about to return. My prayer has been heard. In the precious moments to come I am blessed with a visit of Spirit.

CHAPTER 14

I surrender to Divine intervention

I arrive home just as the sun is coming up. The lake is completely still.

I walk to the front door, thankful to know Wade has a full load of clients today. Since we desperately need the money there is little to no chance he will be coming home anytime soon. For that, I am relieved. I need my space right now. My head is throbbing about as much as my broken heart is. I can hardly turn my neck.

I open the front door, dropping my gym bag right where I am standing, closing the door slowly behind me. Suddenly, I take immediate notice of a distinct silence filling the house. It's beautifully nurturing, seeming to speak to me, telling me it's okay, I am safe. For the first time in months I take in a long healing breath, letting it go into the quiet of the moment.

I place my hand to heart, slightly taken aback by the presence of what I feel and I speak out loud. "Hello?" That's strange I think, "Why did I say that?" My head is hanging a little low as if there is a light too bright to face head on. The light I refer is not physical. There are nothing but clouds outside in the sky. A faint musky sunrise is all that is coming through our floor-to-ceiling windows and there are no lights on in the house. Yet, there is a light brighter than any ray of sun on the sunniest of days.

The Canadian geese are doing their thing, and for the first time in a long time it's bringing me joy. As I allow what is happening to move through me, my world becomes fluid and warm, seeming almost dreamlike. And, as if my body is on autopilot, I turn to the stairs to head up to our bedroom. I was planning on sitting in the living room but something is drawing me upstairs. With every step I take my neck pain begins to hurt less and less. As I enter through the door the clouds outside part like magic, pouring a cascading greeting of the sun in through the window. It awakens a long-lost connection.

Again, I lose my breath. "What is happening?"

Somehow I know the entire room is filled with angels, shining a light that only the soul can see. Their energy is inviting, effortlessly beginning to lift the burden on my soul. *Am I imagining this?* My mind tries to make sense of it. Whether or not it's only my imagination, I am called to accept the lovely invitation the presence is offering.

I close my eyes and whisper aloud, "I am not sure what this is, or if this is *you* … but I feel something here. Something … someone … lovely … and I feel you reaching to me."

I stand tearfully, wrapped in the silence, feeling as if I am being hugged when I hear, plain as day, "Talk to me, Jody, I've heard your prayers. I'm here. I always have been. Turn to me. I cannot do that for you. It's been a long time since you've been aware of me. I miss you too."

I pop my eyes open. A warm rush of energy gently surges through my body. I have no fear. I am filled with joy. What a sweet moment this is! I continue to surrender to the awareness within. The loving presence speaks on, "It's okay to break the silence, you have done nothing wrong."

The kindhearted words are a long-awaited invitation to let go and let God. I effortlessly accept from a place inside I do not ever recall accessing before. It's sacred, deep, and way beyond space and time. I've held my guard for so long the invitation is a precious welcome home. What I hear spoken sounds like a whisper of a long lost friend: "It is safe, Sweet Angel. I know this has been a hard road, and you think I haven't been here with you. That is not so. I have been here every step of the way. You have yet to fully remember me."

Tears begin to well up in my eyes and my heart begins to pound, but not out of fear or anxiety. (I will come to see later in life this is an energetic indicator spirit is speaking with me.)

"There is something you have yet to understand. Something you cannot see through the eyes of physical world understanding. You've misunderstood something, as humans can sometimes naturally do."

There is a long pause, giving space for what is occurring to sink in. "You have done nothing wrong, I have been waiting for this moment. For you to turn to me ... I have been calling to you."

With every heartfelt word the walls around my heart begin to loosen. As I stand in the middle of the room, gently trembling, tears begin streaming down my face. I know I am in the awesome presence of someone sacred. There is no stopping the sweet release of the hurt from the past. Time slows way down. I take in a deep breath, placing my hand to my heart once again, lowering my head and saying to myself, "It's okay ... I can do this ... I can let go." Long-held tears continue streaming down my face releasing the fear and sadness I've been carrying around.

I open my heart further speaking softly, "I've missed you and I've heard you. I am here, I surrender. Talk to me ... " The words leave my lips kissing the soul of Spirit. Permission has finally been granted, and without hesitation the gently surging energy becomes a living light pulsating through me. There are no words beautiful enough to describe the experience. Through a sense not of the physical body I become aware of an elevated world. There is indescribable warmth vibrating through every cell of my body. The warmth goes way beyond that of a fire, or of being under a cozy blanket on a freezing day. It seems to come from a fire within my soul, ignited by way of my authentic surrender. There is no question in my mind about what is transpiring. I am still and know I am. In the divine silence everything is being spoken. Time is suspended. I am shocked by what I hear next:

"Please forgive me."

The words bring me to my knees in uncontrollable tears. I am confused by the request, but the energy behind it calls out to my healing. A few moments pass by.

"I do not know what to say … I am confused … why would I need to forgive *you*? Isn't it me that should be asking for your forgiveness?" The love in this moment is profound.

"Sweet Child, in your innocence lives a misunderstanding of what has transpired. It aches my heart to see you carry this burden as if it were your own. I have been longing for our communion to let you know you no longer need to hold onto it. I know your beautiful heart and I know your loving soul. Your love for me is unwavering and your faith in your purpose lives deeply intertwined with my own. Given the nature of our connection it is easy to assume I abandoned you in your darkest hour. For that misunderstanding I am asking for your forgiveness."

My heart surrenders wide open. As I listen to the words being spoken, there is something running deeper than the utterances I hear. The room is harmonized in energetic splendor filled bumper to bumper with unseen allies of light. I know the intimacy of our connection in the fleshy parts of my heart. My ego mind tries to chime in with disbelief.

Is this all in my head? Maybe it's my over-active imagination? Can I trust this?

Those thoughts are short lived as they are lifted by the undeniable presence of love. It washes through me like waves of an ocean taking with it any doubt or lower vibrational thought. I am now sitting Indian-style on the floor feeling cuddled by a protective cocoon of warm light. The energy is passing through, touching me to the core, continuing to heal the hurts of my past. One by one, wave after wave, they wash away.

I say softly, "I am humbled, God ... and so very thankful." There is a long pause in our communication, giving further space for this to ground. My thoughts become jumbled as I try to gather them in some logical manner. "I still do not understand why it is you've asked for *my* forgiveness."

On waves of compassion and patience the voice answers again. "Sweet Child, by misinterpreting the circumstances of life, the door to truth has been locked to you. Forgiveness is the key that sets you free. I ask for your willingness to forgive in a similar way that an earthly parent asks for forgiveness of its child. It comes from pure love and a longing for your joy. An earthly parent would not want to see a child suffer from a misunderstanding, and I have held witness to your heartache and feelings of abandonment. I seek your forgiveness for the misunderstanding you were ever alone, that you were ever abandoned or that you ever did anything wrong. You are not alone. You never were. I am right here with you. The forgiveness must come from within you." I try to grapple with what I am being told. The voice continues. "I love you so much more than you are aware of."

With that another wave of tears comes to the surface. "I thought you hated me. With everything that went on with DJ ... the betrayal ... the heartache ... the lies."

My eyes sting as the long-held tears leave my body, granting the path to freedom. I can feel the angels standing in a circle around me holding me with love. My ego is determined to fight back the tears, but I cannot. " ... and you see how horrible everything is with Wade. I thought you were punishing me. I thought I must have done something terribly wrong. I was sure you didn't love me."

As I reflect on times past, resentment begins to surface. With a furrowed brow I ponder the mystery before me. I hear the gentle voice again.

"Sweet Angel, herein lives another misunderstanding. With what I say next, I ask of you a little stretch. I know you feel your past has been wasted time. Nothing is further from the truth. Your experience with DJ was not meaningless or wasted time, nor is your relationship with Wade without purpose. Here among the debris lives a rare and beautiful gem."

I feel myself perking up with genuine curiosity. "What do you mean?"

"You are a spiritual warrior by nature and through your experience with DJ you gained priceless tools on your spiritual tool belt. This tool belt is one of your choice and of great service to you and to many others. As I said earlier, if there had been an easier way it would have been so. The experiential aspect is the key to your path of liberation and freedom from self-imposed limitations."

My mind flashes bright, bursting into a living epiphany. My soul recognizes the truth being spoken. *This is a miracle! It's all beginning to make sense!*

I speak again into the love of the room, "I am so thankful it has not been wasted time. The thought of that has plagued me for years. I was certain all my prayers had gone unanswered and ignored."

"I have heard every single one and answered ... only, not in the way you might have expected. You are the gem, Jody. Your inner strength and unwavering courage are extraordinary. Through all that you have been through you've held true to the vision within you. This is a rare gift indeed. Once you are on the other side you will see the blessing in everything that has been, and will be, to yourself and others. Your devotion to the calling of your heart while perceiving no support is miraculous indeed."

I begin to look back in my life and see that it is true. I have always known something, and felt it calling to me from within. I have never been able to articulate what it is. I've only known that it emanates from Love and lives in the truth beyond our humanity.

"Yes, I've always known something. From a very young age I could see the light beyond the sun and even though I was never raised going to church, or hearing mention of you, I have always stayed true to the knowing of the call."

"This is a beautiful thing and I thank you with all that I am for your strength of heart. I know the journey has been rough, not only with DJ but with Wade too. It will not always be this way."

With the mention of Wade's name I burst into tears: "I don't know what to do, God. Things are really rough between us! He scares me and I'm afraid of where it's heading!"

"Sweet Jody, I know your fear and confusion of the things that are transpiring. I've witnessed your questioning of how to make it work as a way of honoring your loyalty to giving your word to marriage. What I say next I say gently. Wade has not the capacity to love you as you are destined to love. Keep the eyes of your heart focused within and I will guide you. In our communion lives freedom."

A slight sense of resistance is passing through me. Even as horrific as things are between me and Wade there is a part of me that loves him deeply, or at least thinks I love him deeply. Maybe it's more accurate to say I am attached. I am caught in a web of illusion, swimming in a sea of red flags assuming this is as good as it will ever get. I have bought into suffering as the only way. I am holding on dearly to what is happening in the hopes of a miraculous change. Not going to happen.

I have gone to such great measures to help us. We're in counseling, where I have made countless attempts at heartfelt conversations both inside and outside the sessions. I have tried to be the perfect fiancé, taking care of everything. I have kept myself small and tried to say the "right" things. I have tried to hug, hold, and reach out to him with all my being, but I've always been met with hostility and rage.

My internal world of low self-worth and no self-love have become a perfect trap. I see no way out. In addition to the emotional dysfunction, I now also have financial dysfunction that tightens the web. I am over $60,000 in debt! It has been accumulated at Wade's request. It was designed to lend additional support to him and his kids with the promise of it all being paid back from his divorce settlement. But the divorce settlement fell through.

Even with all this, the thought of him not having the capacity to love me shakes me. I am beginning to feel desperate.

"No, God. He has the capacity to love me. I know things are going to change ..." My heart is sinking with that thought, but I pursue it anyway, in one last expression of my resistance to the truth and denial of reality. "Please help me ... I am praying for a miracle between us."

CHAPTER 15

And now I walk to the edge

It's been a few months since that beautiful morning. So much was lifted, yet I am still holding on, with a death grip, to the hope that things might work out between Wade and me.

I am in love with his kids. I treat them as my own. The thought of not having them in my life is more of a killer than not having Wade in my life.

Everything is in a downward spiral. I suspect Wade is cheating on me. When I question him he mounts a defensive turnaround, claiming I am making it all up in my head. But my heart knows the truth.

I have taken a job at a credit union where there are loving and supportive people surrounding me, which is a Godsend. I've just completed another day at work and can't stand the thought of going home to him right now, so I have decided to accept an offer from my manager, Stacy, to go for a walk this afternoon.

I call Wade to "ask permission" to go. I do this automatically. It's part of the patterning we have unconsciously created. My desires are placed on the back burner, subject to his approval. When I mention the walk to Wade I can tell by his tone he is not supportive of the idea, but I really don't care. I am growing tired of always doing as he commands.

Stacy and I have picked a walking trail not far from town.

"Thanks, Stacy, for the offer to go for a walk today. It's absolutely beautiful and very much needed."

I turn to Stacy and see a look of concern on her face. She has become a good friend to me.

"Jody, may I tell you something?"

"Sure, Stacy."

I can feel in my stomach she is about to shed light on my current dysfunctional state. She says, "I am really worried about you and your safety. I know you try to keep all that is going on with Wade inside but I can tell things are not good. Are you really okay?"

I have held what's going on so tightly wound in my chest the thought of letting any of it out to someone else feels as if it would consume me. As if she knows what I am feeling, Stacy stops and turns to me, gently grabbing my hand.

She says, "I know what is happening is hard for you and hard to talk about. I also know that me being your manager probably doesn't make it any easier for you to open up."

She pauses, and in the stillness I feel her genuine concern. With a slight sigh she continues as if she knows to give space. "I want you to know if you ever need anything I am here for you. You are a wonderful and beautiful woman, Jody. You only deserve the best in life."

With that, I manage to utter a "thank you," unsure of what else to say. The emotions below the surface are aching and beckoning me to break down and confess my heart to her. The wiser part inside knows I need help. But, into denial I go once again, shoving down what so needs to be set free.

Stacy graciously respects the space my resistance is demanding. She gently redirects our conversation to small talk. It is much appreciated on many levels of my being. There is strange comfort in not seeing the horror before me, which outweighs the freedom offered in the ownership of truth. I am lacking the ability to outwardly acknowledge that what she said about her concern for me and my safety has hit home. But what she said *did* get through. It may seem that the elephant in the room has been ignored, but that is not the case. I have heard her whole-heartedly.

Later, as I am driving home, the precious memory of the walk is beginning to fade. As I near our house, in the pit of my stomach I begin to feel that something is very wrong. Into the driveway I glide, wishing more than anything I was somewhere else. I do my usual internal pep talk: "Things are changing. I'm making this feeling up in my head," all the standard bullshit that has taken its toll on me.

Instead of rushing in, as I usually do to make sure everything is okay, I am taking a moment in the car to notice my feelings. I notice I don't feel safe. My body is tense beyond any measure of what is normal or healthy. I close my eyes, hands still gripped tightly to the steering wheel, and I pray beneath my breath, "God, be with me." The idling sound of the car is an invitation to back this vehicle up and drive away. Go somewhere else, anywhere else, far, far away from here. For a split moment I am seriously considering it.

But the fierce inner voice of codependence and over-responsibility takes over once again. I shake my head and sigh, believing there is no other option but to go in and face whatever may be there. I release my death grip on the steering wheel and reach for the car door handle. "I can do this" I say as I pop out of the car, determined to make everything positive.

As well-intended as my positivity may be, I am sensing it may not be met with mutual enthusiasm on the other side of the door. As my hand nears the door handle, I notice I am beginning to tremble. I suddenly remember the beautiful morning a few months prior when I walked through this same door and was greeted with a great love from unseen allies. I sense the opposite greeting is in store for me today. But I also have a slight feeling that my angels are letting me know they are here with me too.

I take in one last deep breath and turn the knob. I slowly enter into our front entryway.

Why do I feel like I have done something wrong? I went for a walk. This is ridiculous to feel this way.

I am scanning the house to assess what's going on, like a person who is being hunted would check their surroundings for safety. I see Wade standing at the kitchen island with his back turned to me seeming to be looking out at the lake. The kids are watching their favorite show, Sponge Bob, which is echoing its rather annoying tune through the entire house.

"I'm home."

As the words leave my lips I am hoping for a miracle.

No such luck.

CHAPTER 16

The bursting of the storm cloud

Wade whips around from the center isle in the kitchen glaring at me.

"Did you have fun?"

He sneers at me sarcastically with his raspy voice, sending a shiver to my heart. I want to react negatively, but I intuitively know I must not. I try to keep things afloat with a gentle reply, "Yes, I did. It was wonderful to spend time outside in nature with Stacy."

At this point I have walked over to join Wade at the kitchen counter. One look at his face and I can see the rage. He is *really* pissed off. I have never seen him this pissed off. I acknowledge the boys as a means to maybe divert the focus, "Hi Jaden … Hi Lance."

There is an echo of excited hellos back followed by the scurrying of little feet. They didn't realize I was home and have now come over to give me a hug. The welcome-home greeting is short-lived and off they go back into the living room to watch Sponge Bob. I know they love the show, but this time I think they are sensing their dad's tension and want to stay away.

I feel as if I am walking on eggshells. One wrong move and something really bad will happen. I have never seen him like this, and I've seen him in some violent moods. I pull up a chair and sit across from him as he glares at me with a look that could seriously kill someone. He is turning toward the refrigerator, opening it for another beer.

"Is everything okay, Wade?" I ask in meek and gentle voice.

With that the fuse pops. Swinging around to face me, he drops the beer, leans into me, and yells "I DON'T LIKE YOU VERY MUCH!!"

He punches his hand into the granite counter top so hard that is seems the whole house is shaking. Lance, his oldest son, age seven, has run back over to us.

"Dad, you shook the house! What was that?" Lance is halfway laughing and halfway very scared.

Wade sneers at him, "Everything is okay. Go back and watch your show."

I am shell shocked and scared to death. I have no idea where this is coming from or why he is so upset. I immediately focus on keeping calm for fear I am his next target. Gently I proceed to speak. "I am not sure where this is coming from, but if you want to talk about it I think it would be a good idea."

There is only silence, with a sustained death glare aimed in my direction. I try again.

"What can I do to make you feel better?"

Wade is now growling. Literally.

"I don't like you, Jody. Why didn't you answer your phone when you were on your walk?"

His snide emphasis on the walk brings a bit of clarity as to where his hostility is coming from. He doesn't believe I went on a walk! (Later in life, I will see that possibly his over-protective nature and lack of trust was a projection stemming from his own unfaithful actions.) For now, though, I am completely confused but relieved to gradually be gaining an understanding of where the anger is coming from.

With pure honesty I look him straight in the eyes.

"We went walking out on a trail where there is no cell coverage."

How strange is this? We live in the mountains, so he knows the coverage is sporadic.

Wade is grabbing an ice pack from the freezer and wrapping his hand in it to try to stop the swelling. We will soon find out that his hand is broken and requires a cast, but for now he attempts to use the ice to keep the pain at bay.

"You expect me to believe you went walking somewhere where there was no coverage?"

His accusing tone is absurd and getting under my skin.

"Yes, Wade. There are many places around here that don't have coverage. I wouldn't lie to you."

Reminded of what just happened, I catch myself getting an irritated tone and pull the reins in on my behavior.

"Oh, really! You wouldn't lie to me, huh?" His voice is beginning to escalate, matching the glare in his eye.

"No, I wouldn't."

I am continuing to feel threatened by his accusation. I pride myself on my loyalty and honesty, and the thought of his distrust is disturbing.

"Yes you would … !" There is an awkward pause. "You lied to me about DJ!"

There it is, the turning of the knife in my heart. I expected to hear this from him much sooner. Up until now, since DJ's death, all our fights have been about other things and even though I sensed he felt betrayed, he never directly accused me of lying to him. I am at a loss of how to deal with this. First and foremost, my romantic relationship with DJ ended way before I ever knew Wade. And beyond that, my soul is starving for compassion and heartfelt conversation with him. (Two things we have never had.)

"You are such a lying whore, Jody!"

I am shocked by his words. As mean as I have experienced him in the past, this is new pain beyond any measure. The pain is beginning to bubble to the surface uncontrollably. I fear the kids seeing what's going on, once again being impacted by our hurtful words. I turn to Wade with tears in my eyes.

"You have no right to talk to me this way." With that I turn to head upstairs, but before I can go he mutters one last vulgar comment.

"Why don't you go suck that dead man's cock."

With that, the tears begin to stream down my face. I refuse to turn and say anything to him in return. All I want is to be alone.

"Don't you walk away from me!"

He may have a severed vocal cord, but his stern threat is quite obvious, even with only a rasp as a voice. I take a chance and continue walking upstairs. I feel unsure as I proceed but turning to him seems like a worse option.

Oh thank God. I've reached the top of the stairs and can see the doorway to our room. I'm almost there.

I am so relieved he didn't come after me. In previous fights he has been known to come from behind, shoving me and causing me to fall to my knees. I went to work with blood dripping from my leg. I am glad that is not the case today. I know having the kids here is a saving grace.

I close the door behind me, and I grab for the phone to make an all too familiar call to my best friend Jana. I'm hysterically sobbing and want to ask her for help. My calls to her these days are never happy. But she is an angel wrapped in a human body. Never once does she sway in her support. She is always here as my rock and anchor, with generous listening and genuineness of heart. Her love is a beacon of light.

I am standing in the middle of the room with the cordless

phone to my ear. Tears roll down my cheeks. The ringing on the other end seems to be taking forever. I'm afraid Wade is going to come in. I've locked the door as a precaution. Finally, she answers.

"Jana ... " I am sobbing and unable to continue speaking.

"Slow down, Jo. What's going on?"

"It's horrible. Things are really bad. He threatened me and I think he might have broken his hand punching the granite saying he didn't like me very much."

"Oh my gosh, Jody. This is getting scary! Do you need to call the police? Where is he now? "

"He is downstairs with the kids. I think he will leave me alone."

There is silence but I can feel Jana's worry through the phone.

"Jo, are you okay?"

"Jana ... I am so scared ... I don't know how things have gotten this bad. I am so sorry to always call you like this ... "

"Don't worry about that. I love you and I'm here for you."

Her love gives me room for release and sobbing tears come again as I reflect on Wade's words.

"He called me a lying whore Jana, and said I lied to him about DJ ..."

"What? Where did this all come from?"

"I went for a walk today with a girlfriend from work and it pissed him off and when I got home he accused me of lying to him about the walk ... Then he punched the granite saying he didn't like me very much then told me to suck that dead man's cock"

"What?! Jo, this is not okay."

"I don't know what to do."

"You need to *leave* him. That's what you do. This has been going on for too long and he is never going to change. He may apologize and say everything is going to change but it's not. He's *abusive*, Jody."

I bypass what she says, clinging once again to denial just as I did when Stacy brought her concerns up to me. Even though some part of me knows she is right, the thought of actually leaving Wade seems bigger than I am and not a real possibility for me. Ever.

Once again, Jana lovingly talks me through my chaotic mindset with calm and kind words of encouragement. I am left in a holding space of minimal function. I am numb and confused from the waves of emotion. But that will have to do for now. Jana lives over four hours away, so being together physically is not a possibility at the moment. Plus, she has her own life with her husband and three small children. I feel bad for all the time I have already taken from her to tend to my drama. We begin to finish the conversation with my agreement to let her know I am okay before I go to bed.

Like magic, Jaden and Lance are knocking at the bedroom door.

"The kids are here, Jan. I'm going to go. I'll let you know I am okay before I go to bed. I love you ... and thank you again for being here for me. I feel I have no one else I can turn to."

"I am always here for you, Jo. I love you too."

With puffy eyes, I open the door to two little giggling, kind-hearted boys beaming love to me from their hearts and eyes.

"Will you come down and watch a movie with us?"

Their invitation is tempting, given the smiles on their faces. But I am hesitant to agree out of fear for safety in heading downstairs. Yet, I sense enough time has passed for Wade to maybe be calming down. In the past, this has been the pattern. I don't see why it would change now. More importantly, I have calmed down. I feel I can have a rational conversation or at least handle what may come with a little more composure.

I look at the two boys, with all their beauty, and I am reminded of why I endure what I endure. As much as my heart is committed to their dad, as misplaced as that may be, my heart is as committed even more to the two of them. I love them both with all that I am. I grab them both and give them a hug.

"I'll be down in a bit. I'm going to take a shower first."

I know I need to reset myself before facing Wade and something about running water helps me do that. The boys are ecstatic. "Yay!!!" They are galloping down the hallway.

"Dad, Jody will be down in a few to watch a movie!"

CHAPTER 17

Alcohol and mutual dysfunction

As I shower, the glow of the boys' smile and enthusiasm is fading. My chest is tightening in reflection of the evening's events. I seriously question whether enough time has passed for it to be safe for me to go downstairs. I've never seen him like this. Jana's suggestion of calling the cops sits idly by as a valid option. The boys being here is the only saving grace.

The nagging voice of my ego has chimed in with its back and forth ping-pong dance in my head: "What is wrong with me? Why do I stay?"

"Nothing is wrong with you. You can work this out. He asked you to marry him. You're committed."

"I shouldn't be committed! I should be out of here."

"What about the boys? You can't leave them."

With that, I put my face in the hot running water intending to cleanse my soul and shut up the loud obnoxious voice. It's heavy and confining. Distinctly different from the voice of my angels which are voices of light and love.

"Can I do this?" Now the voice of fear joins in. The whole negative committee is in full force in my head. "Can I really go down and face him?" I feel sick to my stomach as I wrestle with my confusion. Now I hear a parental voice, "Sometimes you just need to lift yourself up by the boot straps."

With that I turn the shower off and get out. I go to the closet and grab my comfy clothes, get dressed, brush my hair from my face, and open the door as if I am heading into battle intending triumph. With my chest high and my mind set on peace I slowly walk down the stairs, peering around the corner looking for Wade.

Finally I see him sitting in his chair, hand wrapped in ice, staring at the TV. The boys are on the couch side by side, sharing their favorite play cars with one another. There seems to be a bit of a white flag in the air but I am not yet quite sure.

"Yay!! You're here!" they shout. Wade and I have either done a really great job at masking the tension, or these two little boys are wise beyond their years knowing that joy and anger cannot coexist.

Wade swings his head around and looks at me briefly, only to then swing it back around to the TV. My stomach drops and for a split moment I think of turning around. The boys run off to their room to get a new toy they want to show to me. I know that it is time for me to do my whole *I beg-for-forgiveness, I was wrong, I'll eat all of the negative energy* ritual. I walk around in front of him and start off with something light to test whether he has calmed down as much as I think he has.

"How's your hand?"

There is a slight pause.

"It hurts … I think I have broken it." He has a growl in his tone but there seems to be less aggression behind it. If anything, I am sensing a bit of guilt in his voice.

"Let me take a look." He pulls back the ice pack and I see his hand is purple, blue, and swollen. I take a seat on the ottoman in front of him and reach for his hand.

"That doesn't look so good." My assessment of his energy is accurate. We are in the yellow zone … white flag off in the horizon. I pause for a second before proceeding, hearing the boys in the background rummaging around in their room, eagerly looking for whatever it is they wish to share with me.

I turn my attention back to Wade.

"I am so sorry we are fighting, I don't want us to be like this ..." My tone is calm and genuine. He is now looking at me and softening his glare. I say, "I am truly sorry you felt I lied to you about DJ. I see now I should have told you before but was blinded by whatever misplaced loyalty I was having toward him and our once romantic relationship. I figured since it ended way before I ever met you, it was okay, and I kept it to myself. I am so sorry for that and I wish I could change it all. If you had asked, I would have told you. That was always the agreement." I am attempting to hold onto some sort of inner sense of self-worth and feeling as if I matter, but everything I am speaking does quite the opposite. "And, as for today ... I promise you with all that I am, we went for a walk on a trail where there was no cell coverage. I would never intentionally lie to you. I love you. Next time I will make sure to go somewhere where you can reach me."

Once again I am giving all my power away, begging for forgiveness for something that does not need forgiving.

The boys are back, "Jody, Jody, Jody ... !" They are excited and running full blast from their room in my direction. Jaden seems playfully irritated. "Lance, NO! I want to show her! Not fair!"

Lance is holding something they mutually deem as very cool high in the air floating it around like a space ship. He is teasing his little brother as older siblings often do. I turn to Wade, giving a last pleading look for some sort of completion, knowing our conversation will have to be put on hold. I recognize the familiar "You're forgiven (for now)," look and feel relieved, as unhealthy as that may be.

With an inner sigh of relief I welcome the incoming landing

of Jaden into my lap. They are both such loving little boys. "Jody, look at what we got! Show her, Lance!" He turns to me and once again blesses me with his golden smile. I feel myself lighten up.

"Lance, what is that you have? I can tell it's pretty awesome." He smiles as he holds the aircraft high in the air flying it over some imaginary land I assume is the land of Lancium. "Woooooosshhhh ... wooooshh ... wosh," he gently sails it over into our lap. He leans on me and asks, "What do you think?"

I take the plane in my hands and roll it over a few times with cat-like curiosity. "Hmmm, I love it! Where did you guys get it?"

"Our mom got it for us."

"That was awesome of her, how cool is she?"

"She's WAY cool!" They say to me in unison. I am rather close with their mom, Desiré. She is a stellar woman who often refers to me as a saint. I have yet to let in what she means by that, but every time I hear her say it something inside me stirs. My awareness turns back to Wade who has gone to the refrigerator to get another ice pack and two beers. The fact that he has gotten two beers and not one tells me we could now be somewhat in the green zone. But I never know for sure. I now have both boys sitting in my lap going over every detail of their treasure.

Wade walks back into the room handing me a beer without saying a word.

"Thank you," I mutter with a glance that is begging for *are we are we okay?* I get the green light energetically that we are ... at least for now. I turn back to Jaden and Lance, appreciating their loving innocence.

For a few hours while the kids are awake and the alcohol is low, things remain calm. But after the boys are picked up by their mom, we are starting to pour it on, and my ability to not address what has happened becomes nonexistent. I cannot blame Wade for all our dysfunction. WE, together, are the dysfunction. I have eaten a ton of negative energy that needs to move.

Poke, poke, poke, I go to the sleeping bear: "Why did you say what you said earlier?"

We are now standing around the kitchen counter with a bottle of vodka between us. We are both taking shots. It's not something I am proud of, but at this time it seems somehow wise. Nothing could be further from the truth. Hurt and excessive alcohol is not a great mixture. My questioning springs us into another argumentative go-around that lasts well into the night.

CHAPTER 18

Crossing over into grace

The turmoil of the evening has ended at three in the morning with nasty words and threats that frighten me. I am exhausted, curled up in a ball in the spare bedroom. I have to be to work in a few hours and I'm tempted to call in sick. But I won't. Going there is my refuge.

The hours fly by and it's now 6:00 a.m. and time to pull myself from bed. With a heavy sigh I fling the covers back and slowly walk to the door. I open it, peering my head around the corner to see if the coast is clear. It is. I slowly walk down the hallway to our bedroom door where I intend to sneak in for a shower. As I pass by the bed, I see Wade is not here. He must have gone to train someone. Thank goodness. I quickly shower, get ready, and head out before he could possibly come home.

I drag myself through the door of my work completely ready to drop. I somehow manage to start my day but I am falling asleep at my teller station. My dear friend Tally, who works with me, is sending a concerned look my way. I shoot her a puffy-eyed glance saying, "please don't ask." Thankfully she does anyway.

"Are you okay, Jo?"

I look at her groggily. I can no longer fake it.

"I'm not sure how to answer that question, Tally."

Her big brown eyes filled with love stir up the truth that things are really bad. She sees it. Just like Stacy sees it. Everyone sees it. Yet, I always ignore them. That is, until now.

"I'm worried about you Jody."

I sigh heavy hearted, "I'm worried about me too."

My eyes begin to fill with tears. I have confided everything to Tally. I can't talk to my family. Let me rephrase that: I am choosing not to talk to my family. I have very little communication with them, which is sad, and a first in my life. We have always been very close.

I unconsciously want to hide from my family out of fear and shame. It's part of my denial of how bad things are. Plus, I've fallen into a mind-warped pattern with Wade believing I need to give him ALL of my attention. I realized the other day that the love and devotion I grant him is the love and devotion worthy of granting God! No human being should have this power over another, nor should any human being give this power to another. That is what Wade now has. My power.

Luckily, that is about to change.

This "villain" in my life named Wade is actually a huge blessing and a catalyst for my awakening. It's funny how life works this way. It's the friction that shines the gem.

The credit union is quiet for a moment. Tally and I are sitting at our teller stations talking back and forth, rather intensely on my part, about what has been going on in the last twenty-four hours with Wade. As usual, she is offering generous listening and kindness of heart. As if on cue, I see my manager Stacy walking our way from across the credit union. She is heading straight for me. She stops directly in front of my teller window. Her stance is casual but her eyes are saying something quite different. They mirror Tally's worry and concern.

"Why don't you go take a break, Jody?" Her gentleness strikes a tender chord. "Go get outside for a bit and get some fresh air."

"That sounds like a good idea." I reach for my purse and

grab my car keys. I make a beeline for the door without raising my head to look at either of them. I am afraid of the tears they may see. I am ashamed of my hurt and want to hide it from them, from the customers, and anyone else in sight. I approach the door with a whirling mind, stepping outside into a stunningly gorgeous day.

The air is crisp and the sun is bright. I look up to be greeted by the beautiful vibrant bright blue sky. The breeze is sweet, carrying a wonderful scent of new life sprouting. I am touched by the beauty, for a moment I pause and nothing else matters. I close my eyes taking in the honeyed scent of spring flowers breathing in the air. The peace lasts but only a moment for my seething negative thoughts are powerful and soon take over again. With almost a venomous nature they suck me back into the chaos within.

I feel detached from my body and as I glance at my shadow on the wall I notice a hunched back silhouette being reflected back to me. A broken heart is a powerful thing. It affects the entire body.

I keep my head low as I maneuver through the parking lot, attempting to protect myself from any possible embarrassment. The tears are now passing from my eyes involuntarily. I finally reach my car, open the door, flop into my seat and lock the door. My car is a place I come to often to seek refuge. I somehow feel safe in here. I let out a breath. I wasn't breathing the entire way out.

"Oh my Gosh … what am I doing?" I whisper out loud only to myself. Or at least that's what I think. In complete fatigue and upset, I place my head on my hands and lean myself on the steering wheel. "What am I doing, God?" The question invites the familiar warmth of divine vibrations to fill my car. I hear my angels begin to gently whisper back to me. "We are here with you, sweet Jody."

My awareness naturally gravitates to a conscious connection with their presence. Their impeccable love is gently bringing to the surface what I have been holding back in complete resistance. Not wanting to cling to my hurt anymore I finally surrender in perfect vulnerability. "I don't know what to do anymore, God, please help me. I can no longer do this my way, God, I can't, I choose not to. I surrender it all to you … even if it means leaving Wade."

The permission has been granted for divine intervention. The car is sparkling in soulful splendor. My authenticity in letting go has finally opened the door for Spirit's assistance. I open my eyes and lift my head from the steering wheel. "What is happening?" The world outside disappears for the moment and all I am aware of is an awesome presence of love surrounding me. There is a part of me that knows something has just drastically changed, a miracle has occurred.

CHAPTER 19

When I love you means goodbye

I t is incredible what happens in life when we let go and let God.

God does not occur for me as a religious figure outside of myself. My reference is to the eternal living within. I believe there is a sacred space within each of us where the truth of who we are resides. It doesn't make a difference whether we believe it or not, or whether we are aware of it or not. It's there. It's there with loving intent waiting for us to wake up. As you will soon see, when I let go and let this part of me navigate, miracles happen.

It's been two days since the mystical experience in the car and worldly things are about to go from bad to worse.

It's been another night of brutal fighting with Wade. It's 3:00 a.m. and I am lying in bed in complete fear, confused by who I am and the atrocious behavior that has been coming out of me lately. I would like to say our dysfunction is a one-way street but that is not the truth. I find myself lashing out at him in ways that startle me.

I am curled up in our bed in a fetal position trying not to move. I am so hurt and confused. My thoughts are racing. "What is wrong with me? Why am I even lying in bed with him? Why did I not sleep in the spare bedroom?" All of a sudden I hear a rustle and a growl from Wade as if he heard my thoughts. He has jumped up, and is now flicking on the lights. I lift my head slightly to see he is rushing over to my side of the bed. *Good God what is he doing?!* My bearing becomes completely protective. I pull the covers over my face and try to hide. My mind cannot make sense of what is happening. There's no time. He is ripping the covers back and is now yelling, "My left hand still works you fucking bitch!"

I am stunned. In this moment, as he is standing above me with a cast on one hand and the other hand cocked back aimed at my face, something finally "clicks" inside, and it clicks powerfully. Divine Intervention is in full force. I hear the words of freedom calling to me intently, "Choose me, choose yourself, choose life. Wake up out of this nightmare. You are deserving of love."

In this moment of chaos it is profoundly clear that a door to an answered prayer is opening. I see any further life with Wade is the wrong path. I am not just "getting this" intellectually; I see it with my heart. As he stands here above me in a rage I have never seen before, I look him straight in the eyes and let it all go. I have no fear, only recognition of the beginning of the end and of a new beginning. I feel a loving presence protecting me as I leap into the unknown.

As if Wade knows, he throws the covers back down on me and stomps out of the room cursing under his breath. I don't move. I don't try to engage by saying something. Whatever has clicked is graciously encouraging me to stay right where I am, crying and praying. For the next hour I sit in the silence, wide-awake, hearing only my breath. Somehow, for a few hours, I drift off into some sort of sleep. It's not until three hours later when I wake up and realize Wade is gone, and with that, the shift becomes complete.

I open my eyes, swallowed by the darkness of the bedroom. I take in a slight gasp of air as I rerun the experience from a few hours earlier. The sun is just barely coming up, pouring forth a faint hint of blue light into the room, and even though I have hardly slept, I throw the covers back knowing I have to get up to get the kids ready for school. My heart begins to race. I'm terrified to see Wade. I slowly rise from the bed, grab my sweatshirt, and walk to the bedroom door. The air in the house is chilly, going straight to my bones.

I pull my hoodie over my head and cautiously walk down the hallway. I am aware of every step. The house feels desolate and abandoned. I am wondering where he is. As I pass by the spare bedroom, I carefully peek my head in and see it is empty. I continue to walk downstairs into a deafening silence, hearing only the creak of my footsteps pressing on the floorboards underneath me. I look into the living room to see the chair he always sits in is empty too. *Am I left alone, by myself, to get the kids ready for school? Wow, this is peculiar.* No matter how badly we have fought in the past, we always got the kids ready together, for their sake. This is a first. My thoughts are consumed with how irresponsible this is of him. The lack of communication, at least with his children, is not normal or acceptable. What if I wasn't here to wake them up or take them to school? Standing alone in the entryway, I am forced to see, face to face, the dangerous dead-end before me. If I go any further in this relationship, I will go over a dangerous cliff, with a tragic end.

"Come on, guys, get your shoes on, we gotta go."

Both Jaden and Lance are spaced out in front of the TV. I walk straight up to it and turn it off. "Come on guys ... work with me here." As my hand reaches for the remote, I notice I am shaking. I mask it by quickly turning off the mesmerizing magic light box that sits on our wall. I place the remote in the drawer behind me. The whirlwind of the morning is taxing my nerves. By the grace of God we get into the car and finally head out.

Morning time is never our forté, and given the tempo of today's circumstances it is surprising to me we are leaving on time. I am wiped out on all levels of my being and now worried about staying awake. I have precious cargo in the car and the roads to their school are not fun. We wind and turn and twist through the mountains for forty-five minutes. I silently pray. "I can do this … please be with me."

It's a white-knuckled drive the whole way. There are not many words being spoken. Both boys sense something is very off and give space for me to be an adult. I have made some lame excuse for their Dad not being there this morning. They know it's a lie. My body is aching from the stress of what has happened and of what could be. I shake my head trying to shake off what I am thinking. Where could he have gone? There was no mention of a client this morning. He never trains someone on the mornings when he has his boys.

I pull into the crowded school parking lot. I notice the joy the other parents seem to have as they say their farewells for the day to their kids. I watch their beaming smiles as they give kisses and hugs. I slowly roll past the scene feeling as if I am observing something I will never have. We arrive at our final destination.

"Okay guys, we're here."

I turn around to find them scurrying about the car gathering their things. The contents of their backpacks always seem to magically explode all over the backseat. I sit silently and patiently waiting for them to collect everything.

"Bye Jody, I love you." Lance gets out, gives another wave goodbye and quickly heads to his class. Jaden is the last to get out of the car. In his sweet and endearing way he always prolongs his time with me.

"Bye Jody … " He closes the car door and begins walking to his class. My eyes fill with tears as I watch him walk away. His little back is fully loaded down with an overfilled backpack. *He is such a sweetheart of a boy,* I whisper to myself. As if he hears it, he turns around and waves goodbye mouthing, "I love you." My heart is struck. I begin to tear up.

"I love you too," I say as I wave back to him.

A sinking wave comes over me.

I somehow know this is the last time I will see him.

I try to shake it off but my heart echoes the truth. As I drive out of the school parking lot tears begin to blind me. I am sobbing so hard I can hardly breathe. I am forced to pull over to the side of the road.

The area I've pulled off into is remote, surrounded only by beautiful tall pine trees and breathtaking mountains. Even though I am unable to consciously acknowledge the beauty, blinded by my upset, it is certainly felt and appreciated. The only awareness I have is that I have *arrived* ... arrived at rock bottom, that is. I thought I was here before when DJ died, but now I know that was simply phase one of the great undoing.

Here I sit on the side of the road, a complete mess, unable to move, knowing I am supposed to be at work in an hour. I also know I cannot go. I grab for my phone, praying for cell coverage and see I have one bar. Thank Goodness. I dial the number of my manager Stacy, sobbing, wishing more than anything I could pull it together. I am so ashamed of my life. *Please be there. Please answer.*

I am hoping with all my might she'll answer before the credit union opens. She does, and answers quickly, hearing that I am in tears.

"Oh no ... what's happened? What's going on?"

"It's bad Stacy. It's really, really bad ... he threatened to hit me again last night at three in the morning by ripping the covers off me and then just left, disappeared, leaving me alone to take care of the kids. They are confused and upset. We all are. I have no idea where he is."

"Oh God, Jody … "

"I can't do this anymore, Stacy, I have no idea what I am doing. I keep thinking things are going to get better and they aren't. They keep getting worse. And I'm so sorry, I feel so badly, but I can't come in today. There is no way. I am a total wreck."

"I totally understand, Jody. You need to take care of yourself. I am worried about you … and you know what? Why don't you take the week off, go visit your mom in Fresno and figure out what you are going to do. You need to get away from him."

"Wow, Stacy, I don't know what to say. This is a kind offer but I don't know if I can do that. I'd have to tell my family everything."

"That would be a *good* thing. Say yes Jody. You need a time away to clear your head. You need to let your family back in. This is getting dangerous."

Some part of me knows she is right, and this part is calling to me very loudly. Even in the consideration of her offer I feel myself lighten up to a point where I can breathe. I didn't expect such an invitation, and now some part of me realizes God is at work here taking action on my prayers, flooding me with the courage to move forward and answer the call to choose life—beginning with opening up communication with my family again.

It is undeniable that it's time to let go of shame and let them back in. It's important they finally know what is happening. It's time to get help.

Into the Unknown

CHAPTER 20

There is no turning back now

After my conversation with Stacy, I know it is time to make the long overdue call to my mom, one I suspect she has been anticipating for quite some time. I dial her number, placing the phone to my ear with a shaky hand. I listen to what seems like a never-ending ring.

My mom and I share a beautiful connection. She is one of my best friends and even if I haven't been speaking to her as regularly as I use to, I know she knows something is up. She picks up after the third ring.

"Jody, what's going on?" She is direct but sounds relieved.

Hearing her voice opens the floodgates. I begin to sob.

"Mom, it's really bad ... " I pause trying to catch my breath. "Everything has gotten out of control. Last week, Wade broke his hand threatening me by punching granite telling me he doesn't like me. And then last night, he ripped the covers off in the middle of the night and threatened me again. Now he has just disappeared."

"Oh God, Jody, I knew something was really wrong. I am so happy you have called. I've been waiting to hear from you." I can hear it in my mom's voice, she wants to get in the car, drive to Grass Valley AND KICK HIS BUTT. You don't mess with her daughters.

"I know you've known, Mom. I didn't want to tell you,

that's why I have been so distant and avoiding you. I feel so ashamed."

"Don't feel ashamed. You can always turn to me, Jod. You know that."

"I know I can, Mom." Every word she says begins to free the heavy burden of hiding that I've been living under.

"I need to come home, Mom. Stacy has given me the week off to come be with you and figure things out. Can I come stay with you?"

"Of course you can, any time ... I don't like the idea of you to being around him anymore."

"Thank you, Mom. I'm leaving as soon as I can. I just need to go to the house and get a couple of things."

"I don't think it's wise for you to go back there. What if you happen to run into him? Can you make sure he is not there? Or take someone with you?"

As I listen to her words I am taken aback by the reflection of what life has become. *How did it end up that I am living in fear of my significant other? Isn't he supposed to be my best friend?* A "happily ever after" relationship is what I have always known and envisioned. Some call me crazy or idealistic, but I have always known my time on earth was meant to be spent with a special someone. It is the sacred contract, the carving of the gem, created before we got here.

I know my mom is right. It's probably *not* the best idea for me to go back to the house unannounced. Unfortunately, I know the next phone call I must make will have to be to Wade. My stomach drops in nausea with the thought of it.

Usually, I have no problem calling him, fight or no fight. If you asked him, he would probably even say I call him too much. Today is different. The last week has been an intense eye-opener. The nature of our fighting is headed toward an ugly mess of physical contact. He's a big guy with a background that isn't comprised of much fear. If things push any further, he could go over the edge. I'm afraid the call could be the push.

But thankfully, the fear subsides a little in the knowing I am letting our relationship go, for sanity's sake. I am finally able to recognize the sea of red flags that surround me. For so long I was blinded by them, thinking seeing red was normal. But now the dysfunction is finally too obvious to ignore. The white flag on the hill of my heart is waving clearly in the breeze of destiny. Calling my mom and confessing what's been going on secures my internal commitment not to turn back. It's my nature to be protective of those I love, especially my family. The whole purpose in my distance from them was to keep them in the dark as a means of protection. I refuse to drag my family into this and then turn around and head back into the chaos. One thing that is for sure is once I am done, I am done. And, I AM DONE.

I hang up with my mom agreeing to somehow make sure Wade will not be at the house. She was encouraging me to call the sheriff but I don't want to do that, even though I question if maybe I should.

I sit in my car, holding the phone in hand and staring blankly out the window watching the pine trees dance in the wind. I love the sound of the wind through the trees. I put the window down for a moment to listen to the peace of the breeze. I close my eyes and whisper, "I can do this." I open my eyes, placing my shaking finger on the keypad. "Okay, I'm ready …" I dial Wade's number. "I can do this …" Suddenly, swoosh, like a sudden flash of lightning, a tidal wave of doubt comes over me. It consumes what little courage I had mustered to make the call. I hit the phone's off button and throw it in the passenger's seat. I throw my hands and head back on the steering wheel with tears once again streaming down my face. I begin to seriously question myself. *Am I making a mistake? Can't we work this out?* A blur of utter confusion of past conditioning comes over the morning's conversations with Stacy and my mom.

It's a battle in my own mind between light and dark. I suddenly flash on a conversation I recently had with my dear friend Cheryl. She is a friend I trust wholeheartedly. I visited her the day after Wade punched the granite and broke his hand. We had a heart-to-heart that changed the course of everything. As I sit here in the car, my head spinning with doubt, Spirit is sending a gentle reminder to sway in its grasp. I turn and look at the phone sitting on the seat next to me and hear, "You can do this." Back and forth I go between the clench of the past and the call of a new beginning. I remain paralyzed, staring at the phone. Before doing anything further, I am drawn to remember in detail that blessed day with Cheryl.

I am sitting on her deck facing her eye to eye. I lower my head in shame. She grabs my hand tightly, "Jody, I can't tell you what to do, for I am not you. All I can say is, I have been where you are at and wished I had left earlier. Check in your heart and it will tell you."

I lift my head again to look straight into her eyes. Her gaze is piercing with sheer terror and divine wisdom simultaneously. I feel her soul and the heart of God beckoning to me from a place beyond words saying *you have free will BUT please choose to surrender to the loving will of Spirit.*

The memory of the look in Cheryl's eyes shakes me to the core. I come back to being present in the car again hearing another devoted whisper: PLEASE CHOOSE YOU ... CHOOSE LIFE ... DON'T GO BACK. The power behind the words offers an invitation into the unknown that I cannot refuse. I choose new life and choose to dismiss the voice of my doubt. I look back over at the phone and without another moment of hesitation I pick it up and dial his number. To my surprise, it only rings once. He picks up quickly.

"Hello." Even with the raspy monotone of his voice I hear his panic. From my silence he knows I am done. In every other fight I've called right away in a desperate people-pleasing pleading attempt to take all the blame. Up until now, my pattern has always been to assume all responsibility to try to make things okay. I really believed I didn't matter.

However, this time I do not beat around the bush with him. Like I said, when I am done, I am done. At this moment of arriving at rock bottom I have also arrived at another destination—one of a new beginning.

"Wade, I will not do this anymore. I am done. I am leaving. I am going to my mom's house today, leaving for the week, to figure things out. I can't be with you anymore. We can't be together anymore."

"I'm done too, Jody."

In some odd way, I feel relieved to hear him say that. I sense he is in a semi-regretful state, realizing too this cannot go on any further.

I suddenly remember I am in his car and he is in mine. My stomach drops. I also realize my car has a thing-a-ma-jig in the engine that is currently wrapped in duct tape so it can keep running. My car is literally about to die. There is no way I can drive it to Fresno. My mind races, I go bold.

"I need to use your car. Are you okay with that?" I don't even care if he says no. I will take the train. To my surprise he says okay. So I say, "And Wade, are you going home anytime soon?"

"No, I have clients until 3:00 p.m."

"Good, because I need to go get a few things and don't want to see you."

"I understand … " There is an awkward pause. "And Jody, I am sorry for last night." The tone of his voice is unusual.

I have never heard him like this, nor does he ever apologize. I do not cave in.

"I have nothing more to say to you, Wade." I hang up the phone, sensing immense freedom and tremendous heartache at the same time. I lose my breath as tears stream down my face. I roll the window down to once again hear the calming whistle of the wind through the trees. "Be with me God." I remain seated on the side of the road for a good ten minutes letting reality process.

I am finally calm enough to drive to the house and pick up some stuff.

I am not five minutes into my driveway and look down at my phone to realize Wade has been blowing it up. "That's strange," I think. "He never calls me. And I honestly don't give a crap. We're through … wait, what if he's letting me know he's coming home?"

Out of fear, I check the messages. I want to make sure he is not inside the house. What I hear next is surprising.

The first is a sorrowful attempt to ask me not to leave him. The second is another pleading message asking me to just take a break. The third is an almost-crying message of apology begging me to reconsider. And, they go on from there. My heart is tugged, but I only allow that for a moment. I stay focused on the song of liberation playing in my heart. There is no turning back. The choice has been made.

CHAPTER 21

Some great talks, then a warning

I will come to learn that we create our reality by speaking it into creation. We create by way of thoughts in our head or words spoken aloud. It can be written, envisioned, or sung out loud. Every single one of us is a powerful manifestor, creating our reality every single moment. It's happening whether we know it or not, or whether we believe it or not. It's innate in who we are.

But at this time in my life I am not aware of such wisdom, at least not on the level of the simple self. Yet some part of me knows that I need to talk to those I love as a way to ground my decision to leave Wade. It's not merely for the sake of venting. It's with the purpose of taking the first vulnerable steps on this new path of life.

I am zooming down Interstate 80 starting the download by calling my dad. He, like my mom, is one of my best friends. I'm sure he's been waiting for this call too. As my headset rings through to his number, I flash back to my sister's wedding last year to when he made an honest effort to wake me up to the facts about my relationship with Wade. I remember we had just finished dinner and he was sitting across from me at the table. Everyone else had gotten up so Dad and I had a little one-on-one time.

"Honey, Jod ..." He proceeded cautiously. "How is

everything with Wade?"

I looked up to see my dad's eyes filled with concern. My body language tightened. I looked back down in shame. "Everything is fine."

He knows I am lying. He reaches over and grabs my hand. "Honey, I've been wanting to tell you something and I hope you can hear me. I say this because I love you. I am not sure if you will ever be happy with Wade, or if it's even possible. I'm not sure what's going on between you two, but I am worried about you."

His words send me into complete defense. "We're fine, Dad, just having a little bit of a rough time." My dad senses my wall and lets go a little. "Well, honey … I love you … just know I am here for you." I felt relieved to have the conversation end. But, even though I threw up a wall, I did hear him. His words sunk in.

My dad's voice brings me back to the car. "Hi Honey. It's so good to hear from you." For the first time in a long time I am so happy to hear his voice. The only conversations we have had lately have been brushed-over conversations wherein I tried to hide what was going on. There's no more hiding.

"Hi, Dad."

"What's going on? Everything okay?"

The events of the morning must be obvious in my voice. I am never good at faking how I feel.

"Not really, Dad. Things have gotten really bad. Wade has been threatening me physically."

"Oh no, Honey … Where are you now?" He sounds slightly panicked. I begin to cry and quickly realize it is not safe to do so while driving. The responsibility of the road numbs my emotions temporarily.

"I'm on my way to Mom's. My boss offered me the week off and suggested I go see her … get away and go figure things out. They have witnessed the chaos and are worried about me."

"I'm worried about you too. Why didn't you say something to me, Honey?"

His tone is genuine, gentle, and compassionate.

"I didn't say anything to anyone, Dad. I am ashamed."

With that I get off at the next freeway exit which is random and out in the middle of nowhere in farming land. I pull over to the side of the road where the wellspring of feelings bubbles to the top.

"Honey, you can always turn to me."

"I know Dad. I don't know what I was thinking."

My dad hears my tears, "Are you safe to be driving?"

"I just pulled off the freeway and I'm parked on the side of the road."

"That's good. You're upset and driving while upset is not safe."

There are moments of silence as I try to get grounded.

"Dad, I have something else to tell you."

The looming $60k of debt comes to the forefront of my thought. The debt has been a dark cloud hanging over me. I carry so much shame around it, feeling I have failed. My fear is that my family, my dad in particular, will be severely disappointed in me for being so irresponsible.

Nothing could be further from the truth.

I know that the negative stories we create within our own minds are convincing. But it's important to realize they are stories and not necessarily true. By believing them it is detrimental to alternate options. It shuts them off completely. The story I held about my debt being disappointing to my dad and my family kept me from turning to them and seeking help. The fear of their judgment over the sixty thousand dollars of debt I accumulated with Wade was a big reason for my staying in the relationship for as long as did. I had always hoped he would keep his promise to pay me back.

My dad is attentive with his caring ear, "What do you need to tell me Honey?"

Now I start to panic with the thought of telling him what is going on, but I am willing to jump. Where else can I go? I am at bottom.

"Dad, financially everything is just as bad! I'm sixty thousand dollars in debt!"

There, the bomb has dropped! I finish off my confession with the truth.

I push on, "Wade promised to pay it all back to me. I used my credit cards to support his kids and us. I have NO money Dad. Not even my 401K. I cashed it out to pay our rent for months. He is never going to pay me back. He was relying on a divorce settlement from Chelsea that never came through. And, to tell you the truth, I think he consciously used me, knowing that it was never going to happen just as he never truly intended to marry me."

I begin to feel sick as I look out the window at the dismal surroundings of the road where I'm parked. Inner reality is being reflected outwardly. It's always a precise indicator of what's going on inside. Before my dad can say anything I add another thought.

"And, Dad, I was so scared to tell you because I thought you would be so upset with me and think I am such a bad person. You and Mom have always taught me to be responsible."

The prison bars of my mind become apparent. There really are only two bars with my face so close to them I feel as if I am in a cell. That is not true. I am free at any time. I just need to step back and take a look. My dad's acceptance and understanding shows me that the only one keeping me here, in jail, is myself.

"Oh Jody, I am not upset. This is life and we'll figure this out together. I am here for you and so happy you have finally told me. You can work this out and I'll help you. Life is not over because of debt. The most important thing is your health and safety. Right now it is all about getting you to your mom's safely. Do you need me to come and get you?"

His genuineness of heart touches me. I feel relieved and supported.

"No, Dad, I will be okay. Thank you so much for being here for me. I am so sorry I shut you and the whole family out."

"Honey, we love you."

By the time I pull into my mom's driveway I feel like I am a walking zombie. Unknown to me, she has left work early to meet me when I arrive. I walk to the door with tears of relief involuntarily streaming down my face. Unlike in the past, I don't fight them or make myself wrong for them. I let them flow knowing somewhere within they cleanse my soul. As I reach for the door I become aware of the puffiness of my eyes and what they signify. I think to myself, "This sure has been one hell of a day." I sniffle a bit in my zoned-out space before raising the key to unlock the door. Everything seems as if it is a dream in slow motion. Before I reach the handle, to my surprise the door swings open and there stands my mom with open arms. I let out a long held sigh of relief, walk into her house and collapse into her arms. I am so thankful to see her and so thankful for her hug. I feel as if the marathon of war is over.

As she holds me I leave heartfelt stains of unspoken hurt on her shirt. I have longed for this moment for quite some time. My mom is one of the closest people to me. Keeping my silent distance from her has been an unwanted challenge.

"It's going to be okay, Jody. It's really going to be okay."

She gives a moment of space for my gentle sobbing in her arms. With impeccable timing she pulls back and looks straight in my eyes. I am aware of her hands remaining gently clasped to my arms in a loving gesture of genuine support. "I am so happy you are here, Jody."

The love in her eyes melts my heart and I feel myself let go. The walls I've held for so long are dissolving as I finally let go in surrender. Love is a powerful thing. It is the most powerful force in the universe. For the first time in years I feel safe. Even though my outer world is in utter chaos, I know deep down inside this is the fertile ground of a blessing. My prayers in the car outside my work have been heard and answered. The birth of a new life is in process. Here, at what seems to be ground zero, a new seed has been planted with the divine intention of harboring an abundance of all things beautiful in my life. Just as it takes time for a seed to sprout enough to push its way up through the dirt to reach the rich oxygen in the air, so it takes time for my life to bloom.

We spend the next couple of hours having a tearful heart-to-heart conversation about the details of my reality. I confess the debt, the abuse, and the fact that I have no money saved. For over a year I dreaded having this conversation, and much to my surprise, her reaction was the opposite of what I anticipated. I am being greeted with unconditional love. It's amazing how the universe will support us once we align with the direction of our heart.

It's been a few hours since I got here and I am feeling somewhat calm. It's time for a little logistics. My old room at my mom's is a nightmare of a reminder of the last time I moved back in with her. I was in my twenties, and I'd come back home after a several-year rampage of reckless drug-filled raving and clubbing in San Francisco. The dead old energy of those days is palpable and horrific to imagine living in again. There are old memories of raves where I'd spent forgetful nights, scattered boxes of treasures that I've long forgotten, and pictures of sketchy people I use to hang out with and consider friends, but now can't even remember their names.

My best friend Jana is on her way over to help me change things up a little.

I hear the doorbell ring and feel relieved she is here. She has always calmed my soul when things are rough. I walk downstairs to meet her. She too greets me with open arms, and as I approach her I see tears in her eyes. I welcome her hug. "I am so happy you are away from him, Jod." She whispers her truth in my ear. "I was getting so worried."

"I know Jana. I am thankful to be here too. It was getting scary."

"I brought you something." I notice she is holding a set of bed sheets in her hand. "Feel them, they are like heaven." She gently nudges them in my direction. I reach out to touch the Egyptian cotton and sure enough, they feel like a lovely silk cloud.

"Thanks Jana." My heart is touched as my eyes fill with tears. I know what she is saying. It's her way of letting me know it's going to be okay.

"Let's go give your new space a little love." She gestures to my room upstairs.

Jana, my mom, and I spend the next couple of hours doing a revamp of my old room. We are tossing things out, moving furniture and dusting off the old. Jana has brought throw pillows, a comforter, and soft sleeping pillows for my bed. By the time we are done, my old room is gone. It has been brushed anew by love, transformed into a room filled with an inviting and comfortable vibe.

"There, not so bad, right Jod?" Jana is satisfied with our creation, and coming from her that says a lot. Her eye for beauty is a gift. I am looking at my room amazed at what we have done in such a short period of time. It looks like a totally different space.

"No, Jan, not bad at all. Thank you!"

My mom is surprised too. "Wanna redo the rest of the house, Jana?" My mom's gesture is joking and brings about a bit of lightheartedness. We all giggle a little which feels good to my soul. I am touched by their love and support and become floored by all that has transpired. The tears come again from a place of gentleness and compassion. "Thank you both so much … for loving me as you do. I don't know how I would get through this without you. I know I could have but, well, I am just so thankful for you guys."

They both walk over and envelope me in a teddy bear three-way hug. "We love you Jody. It's time to heal and get your life back. We will always be here for you … no matter what."

With the hustle and bustle of my room complete, my mind begins to stir, drifting to thoughts of Wade.

Jana, as if on cue, picks up on it. "Why don't you come over to my house for a little while Jod? We can order in some dinner and you can see Larry and the kids."

I am thankful for the distraction. I was beginning to get lost in another mental circle of questioning. Jana's husband and kids are dear to me. Their youngest child Kash is my Godson, and their two little girls, Scarlett and Harlow, I consider my nieces even though there is no blood relation. It would be lovely to see everyone and I know it will lift my spirit.

"Sure, Jan … that sounds nice." I turn to my mom. "Wanna come with us, Mom?" She kindly declines saying she'll see me when I get back.

Jana and Larry have a huge L-shaped couch sitting in their living room where I have taken up temporary residency. It's day two since I've been gone, and other than going home to sleep I have sat in the corner of their couch where the two sides meet, flowing between tears and numbness.

I am keeping my cell phone close. It is sitting within sight on Jana's living room coffee table. From the corner of my eye I take an occasional peak, watching for it to light up with an incoming call. I am waiting to hear back from my family. I've left messages earlier today with my stepmom, my older sister, and my younger sister. I am looking forward to hearing from them. I've wanted to connect for quite some time but got lost this last year in the sea of confusion.

I notice that Wade keeps calling, which I am finding rather annoying. For someone who agreed it is time for us to be over he sure is being insistent. I am ignoring him for the time being. I am not even entertaining listening to his voicemail. There is no point. It will further muddle my head.

Hours pass by like dark clouds on a breezy, stormy day. Everything seems dream-like. The TV is on but I do not see what it is airing. I am blinded by my thoughts. I suddenly notice a wonderful smell wafting through the air. I snap out of my train of thought and turn around to see Jana busy in the kitchen fussing about with making something for us to eat. She is dead set on making sure I get something in my system. It sure smells delicious, and knowing Jana, she has cooked up something wonderful. The scent is enticing. So much so, I remove myself from the couch and walk over to join her in the kitchen. In the background there is a murmur of kids playfully instigating one another.

"What ya cooking Jan? It sure smells good."

"It's my mom's chili, the one you love. It will be ready in a bit. You should eat." I know she is right and I can't help but seriously consider the invitation as the irresistible yumminess wafts through the air as it simmers for the next hour.

Jana is good. She knows how to get her way. She wants to make sure I eat and she knows the power of slow cooking her mom's chili, which is handed-down greatness. Even though my appetite is dismal, once it is ready I will somehow manage to get some of her masterful creation into my system. I am in a bit of shell shock from the decisions of my life, which is taking its toll on my system. This Jana knows, hence the creative endeavor to entice my hunger.

Back to the couch I go, full-bellied, left only to the chatter of my mind. Do I quit my job and move here? Do I move out into my own place in Grass Valley? But I have no money. And, I don't want to be near Wade. What about Jaden and Lance? I can't do this to them. What do I do? Round and round my mind goes.

From the corner of my eye I see my phone going off. I am pleased to see it says incoming call from Sharon Sprecher. "Oh, thank God, my stepmom is finally calling me back." I know I left her a message only a few hours ago, but today that feels like a long time.

"Hi Sharon."

"Hi Sweetie, what's going on?"

She, too, has obviously heard the distress in my voice when I left her a message. I can hear her concern and sigh. "Oh Sharon, things got really bad with Wade." I continue to share the details of the horrific sequence of events that has led me to being in Fresno for the week. "I am here, staying with my mom, sorting out what I am going to do. I told Wade it's over Sharon, I am leaving him. I told him a couple of days ago and he agreed." I am very matter of fact with what I am saying to her. In my mind, it's over. We agreed, so that's what is so.

What Sharon says next is surprising, and life changing.

It plays a huge factor in my successfully leaving Wade with grace and ease:

"Be careful, Honey."

"Be careful? What do you mean, Sharon?"

"He will try to suck you back in any way he can. This is what abusers do."

I am confused by her choice of the word "abuser," and slightly startled by what she is saying, but some part of me is calling me to PAY ATTENTION HERE.

"No, Sharon, I don't think so. We agreed the other day it was over." In my mind the words we spoke to one another were words of truth, not game playing.

But Sharon continues, "I understand Honey, but once he has time to himself I think he will be begging for you to come back. This is the pattern of someone who is an abuser. I promise you he will try however he can to tug on your heart chords and get you back. Just be careful and be aware."

Hearing her refer to Wade as an abuser strikes me. How did life end up this way? I flash on the phone calls I took from him on the first day I left before I came down here, and sure enough they were headed in the direction she describes.

"Maybe you're right, Sharon. He's been calling non-stop and leaving messages but I haven't listened to them or answered his calls. Once we get off the phone I will listen to his messages.

"Be careful. I am sure it will be difficult to hear what he has to say. And Jody, don't go back to him. I have been so worried about you. You deserve to be treated with love and kindness. And mark my words Honey, he will say things like *I'll change, I'll go get help, I'll do whatever it takes to get you back*. It will all be smoke and mirrors. He does not have the capacity to change, or love you, as you deserve to be loved. If you were to go back to him things will go back to how they were, if not worse."

I hear what she is saying, but I have a hard time believing Wade would ever communicate this way. He's always been so aggressive.

However, I do not take what she has said with a grain of salt. I can feel the truth in what she is sharing with me. We end our call with her loving words of encouragement, agreeing to talk again tomorrow. I am so thankful for her.

Now, on to the not so fun part, listening to the voicemails Wade has left.

CHAPTER 22

Reassuring voices on the road home

I am standing out on Jana's front porch listening to Wade's voicemails. I feel sick to my stomach.

My hand is to my mouth as I nibble a bit on my nails as a means to unconsciously channel my nervous energy. I scratch my head, shaking it side to side, blown away by what I am hearing.

Sure enough, Sharon is absolutely correct.

By voicemail number six, he is literally begging me to come back, saying he will do anything. I've never heard him like this. He has never apologized for anything that has happened between us, and now all he can say is how sorry he is and that he will change. Everything Sharon said he would say he is saying verbatim.

I am reminded of all the times I asked him to go to counseling with me. He went reluctantly, and was certainly not willing to change or work on things then. How can he expect me to believe he would now? I can't listen anymore and hang up the phone. I can't believe Sharon knew. Every detail. Thank God she told me, otherwise I could have gotten sucked in.

It is hard to hear him like this.

Suddenly my phone is vibrating in my hand, signaling another incoming call. I flip the phone around and thankfully see it is my older sister Samantha. I am so relieved to hear from her. She's always been a tremendous support to me. She too is one of my best friends.

My sister visited Wade and me a few months ago in Grass Valley, witnessing first-hand the magnitude and intensity of dysfunction I was dealing with.

"Oh God, Jody I love those people at your work for supporting you in getting away. I was so worried about you last time I saw you. I didn't know what to say to make you realize the dangerous path you were on. I am so thankful you have gotten away. I wasn't going to let much more time go by without saying something out of my love and concern for you."

She proceeded to tell me how when she visited she found half-drunk vodka bottles in different parts of the house, some in the linen closets and some in the bathrooms. I had no idea. I flash on the night he passed out before dinner when they were visiting. I was embarrassed and let down but did the best I could to have a lovely dinner with them and the boys. I once again made excuses for his behavior.

I continue our conversation. "I wish I would have been open to hearing you back then, Sammy. I was so stubborn and sure things would change."

"Be gentle on yourself, Jod. You've been through so much and really did the best you could." Her encouragement softens me. "Know that I am here for you in anyway I can be. Things will get better. You just wait and see. It is always darkest before the brightest dawn."

Her words are truer than my ego will currently consider letting in.

"Thanks Sammy, I sure hope you are right."

But I'm blowing her hopeful words off as some well-intentioned cliché to make me feel better. I am certain I am doomed, locked down, to carrying life-long shame. Here I am thirty-six years old, living at home with my mom *again* after a failed abusive engagement, preceded by the devastation and betrayal of my shamanism teacher. I am sure I am damaged goods. I have no job, no money, and a car that can drive no further than a few miles without the potential of burning up. I am bogged down with $60k in debt. I know I am heading toward a shameful bankruptcy.

It's not looking very good for the *brighter day* my sister speaks of, but I appreciate her kind words. Right now though, all I see is the dark and dreary landscape of my current reality.

Underneath all of this there is a truth I can't yet see. Below the surface of my limiting thoughts and false beliefs life is preparing me to receive miracles of joy, love, and healing. Even though I'm not consciously aware of it the seed is planted and the soil fertile. I currently do not have the capacity for believing in this possibility, so it stays tucked beneath my conscious thought. Even if I could see what is coming, I'd just deflect it as something I would never deserve. My sense of unworthiness has become fixed as something I consider to be absolute truth. This certainty serves as a roadblock.

Regardless, my prayers were still offered up. And without my realizing it, they have been heard and answered in ways that go way beyond my mere verbal requests. In my offer to get out of my own way and give room for something greater than myself, a door has opened. I meant it when I said, "I cannot do this my way anymore. I give it all to you." It turns out our Higher Source loved the invitation to come in and serve, to "clean up house" in my case. Even in the roughest times in life, times like I am coming through, gifts are given. Where I am is a gift.

What I don't currently realize is that without Wade or DJ I would never be able to be here now having my "internal house cleaned" by Spirit. They are the key to my becoming the woman I am destined to be. They both served my life brilliantly by being the friction and chaos that started the rubbing away of all that is not the truth of who I am.

My experiences with them opened my eyes to the shadow of my soul, from which living in the light was born. We live in a world that is a classroom of duality. Without the negative, I would never have the positive. Without Wade and DJ I would never know the light.

For me, surrender will not be about dramatically "giving it up" with hands held high begging for the universe to take my pain. It's going to be about the willingness to relax, let go, and be receptive with an open heart.

You never know how strong you are until you have no other choice. And I really see at this moment I have no other choice but to go within. There is nothing outside myself to grasp for any longer. I am amidst the death of the old and a rebirth of the new where the Phoenix rises from the ashes.

"Sammy, thank you so much for being here for me. I love you and have missed you. I know it was weird when you came to visit us in Grass Valley … I have so many regrets … "

Before I can say another word she chimes in with an insight only an angel could speak.

"There is no way for you to know what you don't know, Jody." Her tone is gentle and precise. "You have lived as you have lived from the understanding you had. I know you do not want your life to be as it is, but don't regret anything. Life's challenges are what shape us and make us who we are. You're coming through a dark time and headed to the other side now, and that is what is important." She continues to coach me in the wonderful way she does. Our conversation eventually comes to a natural end where I promise to check back in with her in a couple of days.

I shut the phone off and notice I am exhausted. But I also

notice that with each conversation I've had today with those I love my strength has been renewed. I find I have the courage to walk the path before me. I know in my heart there is no turning back, and even though I do not know what is in front of me, I know where I am going is going to be better than where I have been. The choice has been made, and that choice is LIFE.

CHAPTER 23

Unwavering courage and strength

It's been five days since I left Grass Valley and I've made my decision. I'm quitting my job and moving here to Fresno.

The next step is to call Wade to let him know, and my stomach drops with the mere thought of it. I don't know why I feel compelled to tell him. I guess it's a case of misplaced loyalty conditioned by fear of him. What I'd really like to do is bypass all communication with him, but I know that is running away.

Avoidance will not serve the closure and completion that needs to take place.

On a very practical and mundane level, I have to talk to him. I have his car and he has mine. I roll my eyes with worry. I just remembered my car might not even make it down here to Fresno. It's a four-hour drive and my car literally has hoses taped up inside to keep it running. All the logistics begin to spin in my mind. *How am I going to get my car here? How am I going to get all my stuff down here? What about having no money, no job? How will I ever pay off my debt? How will I ever start over with bad credit?* Round and round the fear goes. *And what about the kids?*

With thoughts of Jaden and Lance tears begin to well up in my eyes. I love those little boys with all my heart. As if on cue Jana chimes in, helping to bring my spinning thoughts to a halt.

"What is it, Jo? What are you thinking about?"

She walks over and takes a seat next to me. I refuse to honor my tears. I am so tired of hurting.

"It's the boys, huh?" She knows me so well. Without a word she puts her arm around me. "It's going to be okay, Jo. It's really going to be okay. I know it's hard, but remember they have a great mom. They are loved deeply by her. I know you will miss them and they will miss you, but there really is no other way. You know Wade will never support you in being a part of their lives."

It upsets me but I know she is right. "Thanks, Jan ... " and it's really true. I am not their mom and I'm not even their step-mom. "I know they are loved and will be okay, just like I know moving here is the right thing to do. It's all just hard."

I dismiss going any further with our conversation about the boys. I can't right now. I redirect my thoughts to logistics. "I need to figure out how to make this all happen, Jan." She continues to lend a supportive ear. "I'll need a few days up there to pack the house, but I know I don't want to stay there while I do it. I would have to see him and that is not a good idea."

I begin to wrack my brain for someone to stay with. I feel uncomfortable asking the few friends I have up there. I feel it's an inconvenience to them. Plus, most people I know are afraid of him and I don't want to drag them into the middle of this.

Larry comes to join in on the conversation. "Hey, Jo, why don't we get you a hotel room while you are up there for the few days you need to pack? That way you can have your own place."

At first I don't know what to say or how to receive what he is offering. Larry catches onto my resistance. "It would be our pleasure to help you out Jo," I don't know what else to do. I accept their offer with a humble heart. "Thank you for your generosity guys, I don't know how I'd make it through this without you. By the way, I am going to make it very clear to Wade I do not want to see him while I pack everything up."

We continue to go back and forth about potential options as far as moving my car and personal belongings down here.

As we are speaking my phone begins to vibrate in my hand signaling another incoming call. My stomach drops. I know who it is without even looking. "Oh gosh … " I mutter, shooting a look of fear at Jana and Larry. "I know it's him. I can feel it."

I flip my phone around and sure enough, INCOMING CALL FROM WADE is flashing like a threat. For a moment I hesitate and consider not answering it. Larry chimes in with some wisdom, "I guess his ears are burning. I'd put an end to this now. We're here for you." It's the third ring. I know it's now or never. I walk to the front door to head out onto their porch again. My heart is pounding hard as I answer it.

"Hello?" He responds quickly. "Jody? Oh thank God you answered." I am stunned. Hearing his voice is intense. He sounds more desperate than he did in his voicemails. *Who is this person?*

I cut him off. I'm really intending to keep this simple. "Wade, the only reason I answered is to tell you that I am moving out of Grass Valley and back here to Fresno to be with my family."

He launches into full-fledged begging. "OH NO… pleeeeease don't do this? I'll change. I'll go get help. I don't want to lose you." I am literally baffled by what I am hearing but able, at least at this moment, to keep my guard and remain focused.

"I don't understand, Wade. Why are you saying this to me?

Things have been horrible between us. We had the last few years to work this out. I tried. We even went to counseling. It didn't work. Let go. We are done."

"I know, but I didn't mean it. I didn't mean any of it. I am so sorry for how I've treated you, for all the mean things I've said and done."

Each plea from him is an attempt to chip away at the protective barrier I've placed around my heart. He has never apologized before and certainly never been one to implore forgiveness. Uh oh. Like quicksand, I am beginning to slip into believing he really means what he is saying. I'm even beginning to feel badly for him. "No, no, no … " I say in the back of my mind, shaking off the thought of giving in. I push through.

"Wade, in the past, when I tried to leave, it was met with a profanity-filled, 'Good! Go away!' from you. You *told* me to leave. For some reason, I always stayed. I now have left and there is no turning back for me."

Even as I say the words I can feel myself tempted to slip back into old habits. Part of me wants to believe the con part of his scheme. His seeming hurt is tugging at my old wish for love and intimacy between us. I wonder if I'm making a mistake. *Maybe he can change. Maybe we can work this out.* I shake it off once again and redirect. It is taking all my strength and courage to remain focused on that which I cannot see: the faint whisper promising a better tomorrow. Finally I say, "My only guess is you sensed my lack of seriousness until now."

He bypasses what he knows to be true: I am not coming back. "Please Jody, come home."

"I *am* home Wade. I'll be up next week to get my stuff."

"What about your job?"

"I am quitting my job. And, that's really none of your business."

I can feel myself beginning to boil so I take in a deep breath. I am frustrated by the fact that for years I begged and pleaded with him to get help with me. I was willing to take full responsibility for my part in things. I gave and gave to try and make us work. I even tried to change what and who I was by attempting to figure out how to be the perfect partner, and thus maybe in return he would love me. What I can see now is the victim role never serves anyone. I have finally driven myself into the ground with nothing left to give to us and *he is begging me to come back?* I can't believe it!

I take in another deep breath and say, "I don't want to see you while I am in Grass Valley packing up. Can you respect that, or do I need to involve the sheriff?"

The witness in me is blown away. Am I really negotiating whether or not to involve the sheriff?! Seriously, whose life is this? How did this happen? I ignore the chatter and go on. Now I hear his tears. I don't know if I ever recall experiencing him cry before. He's is not letting this go easily.

"Jody, I love you. Please don't do this."

Hearing his tears strikes the foundation of my unwavering intention. I begin to cry but keep it hidden. I must be strong. I must dismiss the thought that he could ever change. In the background of my mind, I can hear the warning conversation I had with my stepmom the other day. What a blessing. It's serving me powerfully in this moment.

I hold my ground and keep our conversation to a minimum by ending it here.

"I will be there next Monday, and Wade, I ask that you not be at the house while I am there. Can we agree to that?"

The clear request has been made and surprisingly he agrees. I hang up the phone blown away by my courage and strength.

The "people pleaser" in me has thankfully taken a break

but, unfortunately, the doubter in me has not.

The days before I leave to go up north go by slowly, filled with anxiety and restless sleep. Last night was not any different. I awaken once again to an uncomfortable heaviness cloaking my entire body. I pull myself out from under the covers and plop myself down on the edge of my bed. I am feeling paralyzed by the thought of driving to Grass Valley tomorrow.

Talk to me, God. Am I making the right choice? Doubt is swinging in like a sledgehammer to reality, taking its toll on every ounce of my being. *God, I don't know if you can hear me or if you are even real but this is tough and I need your help. I feel caught between the pull of Wade's convincing plea for change and the calling of my own soul to break free. If you can hear me I am asking for your guidance.*

It's about 6:30 in the morning. Stormy clouds are greying out the blue skies. I feel sick to my stomach thinking of what is to come. I've made the mistake of humoring a few calls from Wade the past few days. Not the wisest of ideas. My head is muddled with empty promises. He is now using his kids as leverage for another attempt to get back together. I find myself in and out of moments of serious doubt, questioning whether I am making the right choice. *Do I have what it takes to get through this? I seriously have no idea if the calling I hear inside is even true.*

My heart sinks, thinking I am speaking only to the air, but before another moment passes the answer comes.

Sitting here on the edge of the bed my intuition has spontaneously heightened, opening the channel to my heart. I begin to hear words that are distinct, kind, and caring, "Sweet Angel, thank you for turning to me. You are well equipped to handle that which is before you. Trust in the strength of your heart and the wisdom it shares with you.

You are stronger than you currently know and the brighter day your sister speaks of is it not far away. Preparation is in motion. This is all part of the process."

I take in a quick breath, a little startled by what I am hearing. However, there is no fear, only an undeniable sense of love. The voice seems to be coming from a gentle stillness within. I sense energetic patterns of undeniable insight. I place my hands to my heart as the heaviness is miraculously lifted. I feel light and free, without the presence of doubt. I am humbled.

The voice continues, "You're not alone. I love you. You may not be able to see me with the eyes of your body but the eyes of your soul know me and know I am here … I have always been here with you." I now begin to feel tears of joy sting my eyes. "Your body is a temporary temple that houses the truth of eternity. It will someday break free from the restrictions of earthly reality shining light on the truth of which I speak. You are love and you are loved. This is all part of the journey."

My body begins to tremble. Every cell is filled with delight. Outside, the once-grey skies have broken up and are now trickling into my room an array of bright playful sunbeams. It's as if I am receiving a direct hello from above, bonding the angel's imagination with mine. My sixth sense opens where I recognize my spirit lifted in balance. Rather astounded the only thing I can say is, "I think I am crazy … I really do. But, some part of me knows that is not true. As I sit here having a conversation with you it feels so familiar, so loving and all knowing, like home to my soul. If I ever *told* anybody they would probably call me bonkers." With that thought I close my eyes and pause, leaning a little toward doubt. "How is this possible? Am I losing my mind?"

The loving gentleness does not sway, "In truth, it's quite the contrary. You're finding your way. An opening has occurred making all things possible on the wings of the Divine. This is not meant as a religious cliché. What I speak of is outside of religion for religion can consist of separation. What I speak of is whole in perfect union, and that union is Love. Your broken heart has led to an opening, a crack that has let the light in. That light is living … that light is love … you are that light. You are LOVE."

The beauty of what I hear blows me away. I surrender. My little self-ego cannot deny the wisdom and knowledge present. In the stillness of the moment, I flash to the last few months and the sequence of events that have transpired to bring me to the now. Had it not been for the experience of the phenomenal visitation at Wade's house after the devastating day at the gym, or the prayerful communication in my car where I surrendered, my life would not be redirecting as it is.

CHAPTER 24

Country roads take me home

Yesterday flew by. I am now on the road, driving north in the silence.

The back country roads are twisting and turning. I pass by a giant oak tree and out of the corner of my eye I see the leaves dancing in the wind. The sun is trickling off them in flashes of brilliant light and for a moment I feel peace. Nature, and all her beauty, have always had a calming effect on me.

I'm finally driving into Grass Valley. It's about noon, an hour later than I said I would arrive, so I figure Wade is long gone from the house. He knows my approximate arrival time and agreed not to be here. I am trusting he is going to keep his word. My internal tape continues to spin however, *Is he going to do anything crazy? I just want this all to be over. I'll never let anyone into my heart again.*

I see the entrance to the driveway and slow down to turn in. His house is at the bottom of a long and windy driveway stretching for about mile. The driveway lands right at his house on the water. This was once a welcome sight, but now I feel as if I'm in a bad dream. I can't wait to get back to Fresno.

"OH MY GOD!" I gasp as I slam on the breaks. My stomach drops to the floor. It's Wade! Red flags cloud my vision as whistles of warning are tooting off in my head. If I could throw the car in reverse I would. It's too late. Go figure that the universe would have it that I turn in just as he is just turning out. If I'd arrived even a minute later this would not be happening.

He jumps out of the car with a clear intent to talk to me. Out of my confusion, I also get out of my car. He rushes up to me and gives me a hug.

"Jody … I miss you … please don't do this."

I am startled and pull away, "Wade, let go. It's over."

It's truly difficult to see him. It's taking every ounce of my personal power to ignore the fact that my heart hurts deeply. He looks like he has been through the ringer. He is shaking from head to toe, and looks as if he has lost at least ten to fifteen pounds.

He pleads, "I can't be without you. I miss you terribly and the boys miss you too."

There he goes again playing the boys card. UGHH this is so hard! Mention of the boys is a serious tug on my heart. I can't go there. The only response I have left is defense. If it's not defense, it will be meltdown. And that is not an option.

"Yes you can be without me. Don't do this, Wade. I cannot talk to you right now."

By some amazing hidden courage I continue to stand my ground. He tries to hug me again. I withdraw from his grasp avoiding looking into his eyes. I turn back to the car, "I need to go pack some stuff but if you're planning on being here today I will come back tomorrow." I intend to shut the car off and give him his keys. I figure now is a great time to trade vehicles.

There is a messy exchange of jumbled words between us ending with Wade getting into his car and me getting into mine. He reassures me of his agreement to give me space to do what I need to do. He isn't happy about it, but he now understands that there is no moving me.

That was the last time I ever saw him.

As I wind down the last part of the driveway, attempting to throw off the last few minutes of my conversation with Wade, my clunker car is causing some concern and anxiety. It's making all sorts of strange sounds and vibrations. *How in the world am I going to make it down to Fresno in this thing? That's four hours away.* I find peace in remembering that my dad is on his way. He is flying out from Nevada to meet me here, and has offered to come drive the U-haul down to Fresno while I follow him in my car. I take a breath and let the worry go.

The once-welcoming sight of Wade's house now seems like a nightmare. I get out of the car and immediately look out at the lake. It once brought me peace. Not today. I don't want to be here. Resistant and resentful, I open the front door. It feels as if I am walking into a bad dream. A shiver runs up my spine. *I use to love being here … Has it only been a week?* I question the possibility of it seeming like an eternity, but I know that's not truly possible. I know when I was last here. The house now seems foreign, like I am walking through a graveyard. *Keep your eyes on the purpose.* I remind myself why I am here and get a move on with what needs to be done.

Three days is what I've given myself to pack up everything I own, but oh my goodness! These three days have been consecutive days of holy hell. I am finally done with the upstairs and have left it sparkling clean for Wade. Why? I don't really know other than that's my style. I walk downstairs with the last packed box and load it onto the U-Haul trailer. I throw it in, pushing it back against the other boxes while letting out a big sigh. Exhausted, I take a seat on the tailgate and wipe the sweat from my brow. "Almost done," I say to myself.

A gentle breeze comes up from nowhere, capturing my attention. It's soothing to my soul. Strands of my hair are playfully tickling my face and for a moment I let all the frantic energy go. I look up into the sky and see brilliant bright blue being kissed by fluffy white. It looks like scattered cotton balls are filling the air. My imagination gets lost in their nothingness and in this moment it seems that nothing else matters.. I close my eyes and listen to the breeze through the trees. My artistic nature is appeased.

The moment of peace doesn't last long. It's quickly halted by worry. Any sort of hope these days is always jerked right back to that. I have yet to learn that I can choose my thoughts. For now I am consumed by fear. *What am I going to do?* A negative fantasy begins to take over. I have spent ten grueling hours a day for the past two days going through every inch of this massive 4000-square-foot house. I have been wading through stuff that has triggered past memories. Resentment is fueled for what seems like a life gone wrong. The images of a doomed life are flashing in my head. Everything looks like utter chaos. I look up into the sky once again wanting to climb aboard the clouds and float away, but that is not going to happen. I know what I need to do. I look back at the front door and let out another sigh. "I guess I better get this done." I get up from the tailgate and head to the door. I have temporarily forgotten the divine conversation from a few mornings ago. But luckily it has not forgotten me.

As I enter back into the house I hear gentle encouragement coming from within. "You can do this. You are stronger than you realize. When one door closes another is opened. Energy is neither created nor destroyed, simply transformed. You are in the middle of transformation." Once again, I am reminded that I am not stuck.

I try to deflect what I hear telling myself it's just my over-active imagination. My free will once again gives way to retreat, back into the more familiar thoughts of feeling cursed by God. It's amazing how I have become comfortable in my misery.

I begin to scan the downstairs, trying to figure out where to get started. I've done a lot of it already but there is quite a bit more to do. "I just want this all to be over." This saying seems to be my mantra. My heart feels so heavy I am finding it hard to breath normally. I am continuously sighing unconsciously in an attempt to get enough oxygen into my body. All of a sudden I am startled by hearing a car outside. It's coming down the driveway. My stomach drops as I swing around and head to the door expecting to see Wade. Bug-eyed and fearful I peer my head out the door and look down the driveway.

"Oh thank God! Hi Dad!"

I turn around to see him getting out of his rental car. I walk over and greet him with a big hug. "I'm so happy you are here."

"Me too Honey. Wish it was on better terms. Looks like you've made good progress." He is gesturing to the open U-Haul already filled over halfway full. "Need any help with anything?"

"Actually, I sure do, your timing is impeccable." We spend the next few hours packing up the rest of my stuff, loading furniture and boxes into the U-Haul. Finally we arrive at the last box. "Well, that's it Dad. Let's close her up." I have a mixture of feelings going through me as I walk to the front door to return the key to Wade. We agreed that I'd place it under the mat on the front porch for him. My dad is rolling down the gate to the U-Haul and as I hear it latch everything becomes surreal. "We're locked, loaded, and ready to go," I hear him say from a distance. My stomach drops at his words. "Am I really doing this?" Tears once again stream down my face. I have no idea what is to come. All I know is I am walking away from the only place I thought my heart could be and walking straight into the abyss of the unknown.

Recognizing a blessing when it feels like loss is not an easy task. At this point of the journey I am unable to see what is truly transpiring. In a few years, when enough distance has been gained through healing, I will see this time as dear, and how it created the life of possibility.

CHAPTER 25

A white candle and an open journal

It's been about a month since I moved back to Fresno from Grass Valley. Even though I have had ample downtime, what I have been putting myself through in my own head has taken its toll.

I now wear guilt as an absolute truth of who I am. It is such a big a part of my thought process that it feels welded to my identity. I have firmly cemented the false belief that I don't matter.

I feel my world is at a dead stop. I find myself worrying about my future almost all the time. I'm living with a constant sense of urgency. I wake up with anxiety. I am scrambling about looking for a job. It feels as if I'm in a constant mental boxing match. I am certainly not being gentle with myself. Nor am I acting with any self-love. I do not know how to.

Maybe it's because I still feel like a failure. I see no movement on the countless resumes I have sent out. I have met with every job placement agency in Fresno and nothing has come of it. What is currently going on is I find myself inside a great lesson about surrender (even though I don't know that's what's really happening.)

The one positive aspect of my life is that I have opened communication with the Divine again. Every day, I am engaged in conversations, even though I usually dismiss them afterward as overactive imagination. Regardless of my disbelief, I continue to have them. They bring insights and support that are comforting and profound. I figure since I am growing in ways I could never have imagined, who cares if I am talking to myself? It's become a morning ritual to spend time with this inner guidance.

Cuddled in bed, I open my eyes and see the sun piercing through the blinds, seeming to emanate a promise of a better day. Like a trickling waterfall of hope, there is an inner sense of recognition. I try to quickly dismiss it and turn instead to the familiar thoughts of stress that run me these days. My stomach flutters as the static nature of my mind takes over, bringing me down to what I believe is "reality." I pull myself out of bed and stumble half-asleep to the bathroom. I feel heavy again in my body. I lift my toothbrush to my face. I'm taken aback by the reflection staring back at me. *Good God. I look like a Mack truck has run me over. When is this going to end?*

I brush my teeth and go back to my room to take refuge. I am surprised to notice there is a lovely energy in the room. I light my white candle, as I do every morning lately, and grab for my journal. I don't know what else to do other than turn inward. For the last month, every morning before I start the mad dash of job-hunting, I spend time in inner reflection.

Today is no different. My pen is in my hand as I write, "Good Morning, God. I need your help. I can feel something. I felt it this morning when I opened my eyes and the sun was speaking to me. I think I am crazy but what am I to do? I can feel you trying to show me something and I am not even sure if you are real. I am confused."

I let the words flow from my favorite purple pen. I begin to sense the familiar warmth I get from communion. My room is filling with light. I still try to dismiss it all as mere imagination. Like I said, to this point, I have no belief in whomever it is I am talking to. I am almost certain I am making it all up in my head. Even when I mention "God" part of me doesn't really believe it. My past casts a shadow on everything. I don't fully trust the possibility. But I continue to open, little by little. And as I allow myself to open, what comes through feels sacred. It's kind, loving, wise, and supportive. So I let it flow in.

"Sweet Angel, I encourage you to be gentle on yourself. You will soon see you've turned the corner. I know it's hard to trust the process given all that you have gone through. I am here with you and your disbelief does not change that. Where I originate from is Absolute Truth, and no amount of humanness can change that. I acknowledge you for your inner strength. The Path that you are on is not for the faint of heart but is well worth the effort. My love for you runs deep … deeper than you yet remember. Enjoy the down time you have right now. Soon it will be GO! AND when it's go, it will be full on."

CHAPTER 26

Do I want to be a flight attendant?

D ays roll by, one after another, with no movement on the job front. I find anxiety is my constant companion. It especially rears its head at night as I grapple with making sense of where I have landed. I continue to pray, asking for guidance, and tonight is no different.

Before laying my head on the pillow I take a moment to ask a pointed question.

"Why am I here, God?"

I do not wait for an answer though. Instead I go to bed. From the standpoint of my ego the question is rhetorical. Once again, my disbelief has taken over. I constantly question whether or not I am speaking only to the wind when I pray. Luckily for me, the great thing about dream space is Spirit can come through the door the ego blocks out in waking life. I have experienced two different types of dreams: those of processing and those bearing a message. The latter has made several life changing appearances, and tonight will be another.

It's 7:00 a.m. I sit up in bed. I just had an amazing dream! This is the first time in a long time I have felt inspiration. The remnants of the dream are quickly fading to black, but the tones of the message are not. I am being guided and even though I may be left imageless the positivity is pulsating vibrations through my body, surging like a high voltage wire connected to Heaven. It's as if I've tapped into communion on steroids: *Flight Attendant! That's what I want to do. I want to be a flight attendant. I love to travel. I love to journey to far off places. I could do that for a living.*

I can hardly get out of bed fast enough. I grab my very old, hardly-working laptop and sprint off to the coffee pot. I have one hand opening the ancient device and the other fumbling around with water trying to get the pot ready for coffee. "Come on, come on you silly laptop." This old school device really needs to be put to rest. Finally the internet browser pops open. "Thank God."

I type as quickly as I can: *How to become a flight attendant.*

After a few painful minutes several websites pop up. I dive in and soak up as much information as I can. *Hmmmmm, I am not quite sure I'm feeling this. It looks like it would take too much time until I'd be flying in the big planes and that's what I'd want to do to. That's how I would journey to far off exotic places. And, it seems there isn't much of a guarantee of how many hours I'd be working.*

I begin to feel slightly deflated. But suddenly, out of nowhere, I remember a conversation I had with a lovely woman over two years ago when I worked as a teller at First US Community Credit Union. She was amazing! She strolled in to make a simple deposit, beaming with light, sharing her beautiful energy with me. Our conversation quickly and naturally gravitated to things of a spiritual nature. I remember instantly feeling a natural inner connection to her.

"You know," she paused, scanning my face in honor of our connection, "have you ever heard of the University of Santa Monica?"

"No, I have never heard of it."

"I think you'd really love it. The education is exactly what you are talking about. You speak their language with what you are saying, especially when you mention believing we are Spiritual Beings having a human experience and not the other way around. That is the basis of their entire coursework, that and compassionate self-forgiveness. I'm going to bring you in a CD tomorrow so you can check it out."

I feel ecstatic! We complete our conversation and after she leaves I take a quick break to look up this *University of Santa Monica*. Oh my goodness! With each word I read on the University's website I began to tremble with excitement. *Finally! This is what I have been looking for. I know this is my calling. I am so happy she came in and told me about this! This place really does speak my language.*

When I graduated from college in my late twenties with a Bachelor of Arts in Psychology I thought for sure I would never continue on with a higher education. I distinctly remember telling myself the only way I would ever consider it was if the University took into serious consideration the Soul. I didn't really believe a place like that existed, so I let the desire go.

My undergraduate work consisted of long lectures, evaluations, and psychological tests suggesting the data given gave shape to who a person was. That never fully resonated with me. I have always known we run much deeper than that. I recognized on some level we couldn't completely know another, or ourselves, from matters of the psyche only. To truly know who we are is to access our essence beyond humanness. It is to awaken and embrace our true nature, the one where our heart and soul come home in recognition of the truth that we are Love. The wisdom I speak of is the basis of the education I have always sought and longed for but thought absurd for considering possible. I always believed in an enlightened education, but thought it was a far-fetched ideal.

Now, here I am reading the words I've waited so long to read. *How cool is this?! A private university that teaches a Soul-Centered education! This is what I have always hoped was possible.* The positivity is short-lived, diminished by heart-sinking thoughts: I am face to face with what seems an insurmountable obstacle to overcome, my own fears. My enthusiasm quickly spirals into panic. "I can't do this. First, I can't afford it. Wade and I can hardly make our house payment. Oh gosh ... and then there's Wade ... he would NEVER be supportive and on board with this even if by some miracle I could get the money ... he doesn't like me to go anywhere and who would take care of his kids ... and then there is the travel. There is no way."

Fully deflated I let the whole thing go. Poof, into the air. Or at least I thought. That is, until NOW. This morning the University has circled around again by way of last night's profound dream of being a flight attendant. Ping, pong, my thoughts go. *I really did love that school. But I definitely can't go now! Even though I'm no longer with Wade, I still have no money, no job, no car, and I'm up to my ears in debt.*

Then I hear a gentle nudge urging me to return to the University's website again for a quick second, just to visit it and check it out for fun. Tapped back into the flow, I click, click, and click away. Up pops the University of Santa Monica website and once again, two full years later, my body begins to fill with excitement. Like the sweet smell after the first rain it all comes back to me. The inspiration I awoke with is taking on a whole new level of meaning. *Wow ... that's right! This is my calling!*

Something begins to stir in the direction of how true that really is. I spend hours soaking in the content of the website. The reality of my path begins to set in: *I would love to go to this school. But I can't. There's no way.* I am in a boxing match with my own limitations. The gentle stillness seems to be proposing otherwise. But my doubts continue, *if I remember correctly it's REALLY expensive to go there.* I quickly navigate to the payment page. *Oh my ... good news.* The light bulb goes off! Ding, ding, ding! Right way! *Hmmm, it is not that expensive after all, and if I were not in my current situation it's actually very reasonable.* It's funny how our egos work out of what appears to be protection to scare us out of our heart's desire. I continue to scan the payments page as sparks of delight begin to bubble up like divine popcorn: "The University of Santa Monica has a monthly payment plan."

I begin to see that this really could be doable! And doable NOW. *Hmmmm ... I have just enough money to my name that if I were accepted into the program I could cover the first month's payment.* However, this line of thinking is not going over well with the inner critic. It begins to speak up, "Are you crazy?! What would your family and friends think? How can you even think this? You have no job, you're in debt, you have no functioning car, and you're living at home with your mom."

My small-minded ego is throwing a convincing case for how there is no way for this opportunity to be real. Luckily for me, however, my soul is navigating this ship. I click over to the Admissions and Next Steps page and see that class is starting in October. *I need to be there!* If it starts in October, that gives me more than nine months to find a job. I can't believe it, but I am serious about this! All of a sudden I flash on my dream from last night. Like a movie screen, it snaps synchronistic images into my mind bringing clarity as to the meaning of the dream.

"Ohhhh!" I say out loud giving a loud giggle to the air, "Flight Attendant ... " I have a smile from ear to ear. "I get what you mean now. You're good, God. I love that you have a sense of humor. I see how attending this University would be like attending a Flight Attendant School for the Soul." With waves of playful energy tickling in my belly I hear clearly from the still small voice within. "I'm so happy you're able to see with the eyes of your heart the symbolism sent your way. Regardless of your acceptance, you're about to take off on a journey unlike any other. Trust in your inner knowing. This flight is beyond any you could imagine. You are meant for a great journey on the plane of Wisdom. Take a chance and climb aboard. You are destined to become a Flight Attendant for the Great Divine. The process of ushered awakening will inspire others to climb aboard and learn to fly."

As the excitement is pulsating through my body, I quickly click on the application and print it out. I begin to read it over and, uh-oh ... SLAM. Back down to doubt I go. "Oh my God, I can't do this!" This time money has nothing to do with it ... it's question number five from the Psychosocial section of the application. It reads: *Please describe any challenging events or situations you may have experienced (including, but not limited to, abuse, violence, chemical dependence, divorce, anxiety, or depression)*

Oh my gosh I have or have had *all* of them! Well, maybe not divorce but close to it! My heart begins pounding. *I could NEVER tell anyone what has happened to me.* I quickly dismiss thinking any further about filling out the application.

But like a magnetic force filled with some sort of magic mojo, I find myself standing in the middle of my room unable to redirect my thoughts. My hand and heart remains firmly gripped to the application.

I hear: "Breathe, Sweet Angel ... just breathe."

CHAPTER 27

Finding help to leave the hole I'm in

I walk over and take a seat on the couch. I sit staring blankly at the application in hand. My body is trembling so much it's shaking the pages. I really don't know what to do. I close my eyes and hear welcomed guidance: "Inhale. Hold for a moment. Exhale. Inhale. Hold for a moment. Exhale."

With each breath I calm down, and sure enough tears begin to well up in my eyes. Question number five is freaking me out. I am carrying a tremendous amount of guilt, shame, and blame for my past, and this question, asking me to describe any challenging events or situations I may have experienced, has rattled the cage of fear.

I am holding onto my resistance with a death grip. I do not want to answer it. I hear gentle encouragement come through again: "You can do this. You're not alone nor are you to blame for what has happened. In this, there is a great opportunity for healing and freedom. Your strength of heart is great and you do not walk alone in this. We are with you. The essence of who you ARE is courage. Be confident in this and walk toward the call of your heart."

I am soothed by the kind support and take another deep breath. I see I am face to face with a choice.

I can choose new life or I can choose to remain in misery.

I feel I am standing on a cliff within my own consciousness

hearing the angels beckoning me to jump toward new life. They are standing by in love, reminding me I can fly. I feel their inspiration surge through me, gracefully taking fear with it. *I can do this! I can!* With that I boldly stand up and walk back over to the counter and flip open my barely-functioning computer and begin the application process. It will take me two weeks and twenty-one pages to complete.

"You're doing what? A masters program?" Larry looks dumbfounded by what I am telling him.

This has been a common response among those I love.

Jana, Larry, and I are standing around their kitchen about ready to order take-out for dinner. I am nervously fumbling with the menu using it as a distraction from the perceived judgment I feel. I look up and see the look on Larry's face. It's one of sheer disbelief, and one that says that I may be a little insane. He approaches his next line of logic in the gentlest way he can.

"Don't you think that maybe you should consider getting a job and getting out of debt before you apply to a masters program?"

I know his concern comes from love. He's a successful businessman and holds a logical view in the world that has served him well. I respect him highly, so his challenge to my choice is a little troublesome.

"I know it sounds crazy," I say to him, " … and I can't explain it, other than to say I know I am meant to be there."

I look over at Jana who is busy with the kids. I really want *one* of them to tell me they support my choice! But, then again, my track record for good choices hasn't been the best up until now. Energetically I get she is in the same boat as Larry. The one that thinks I am a tad crazy.

Spending the last two weeks writing twenty-one pages to complete the application might seem a little excessive, yet I find myself lost in a process of deep self-reflection. Even in the presence of tremendous fear, I am somehow experiencing a spiritual awakening that has put healing into motion. The process of sorting out what I was willing to share with others seems to have started the great undoing of old hurts and crushed dreams. I have answered the questions with total vulnerability, which is surprising since I tend to be guarded.

My willingness to be honest has created a profound opening to inner freedom. I've had flashes of insight that have generated new possibilities for me. One being that maybe I can really heal. I never knew I had such courage. What I have shared in the application are questions I swore I would never share with anyone! I was determined to carry my unresolved material around for life. (Not a particularly healthy choice.) In the ebb and flow of resistance and surrender healing has miraculously taken place. Like the pulling of little thorns from an old wound, I slowly begin to mend my bruised heart.

"It's done!" I am literally running down the stairs heading full force toward the table where my mom is sitting with her cup of coffee.

It's a Saturday morning and for the last hour I have been reviewing what I have written on the application. My skin is slightly damp from the anxiety I have about its completion. It's painfully clear that there is nothing further to say or add. I say painfully because I now face the really freaky part: the reality of mailing it off!

For a moment, I begin to doubt again whether I can do this or not. But before I can get too caught up in my fear my mom chimes in with what feels like a message from the angels: "I'm so *happy* for you Jody! I know filling this out has been a challenge for you. Even though the timing of applying seems off, if you get accepted I feel it could be a great thing for you."

Her words surprise me. Usually she wouldn't encourage such a leap of faith. Especially since I am living at home with her with no job. She'd usually be on the other side, where Larry and Jana are temporarily hanging out.

But out of everyone, my mom seems the most onboard with this unusual, bold choice I have made. I can't help but think she secretly hopes USM will help me crawl out of the hole I am in, both inwardly and outwardly.

CHAPTER 28

You've got mail

I t's been a couple of months since I applied to the University of Santa Monica and still no word.

And, still no job.

Every day I walk to the mailbox to check the mail, and everyday nothing arrives. I am becoming more and more discouraged and embarrassed, finding myself wallowing in pity and self-loathing. *Maybe I made the wrong choice. Maybe I'm too messed up and got denied because of my horrific past.*

At some level I realize what I am thinking is not true and that it's only my ego playing a game of doomsday negativity with me. But at this moment, that's not clear. I believe the thoughts are true. I'm having a hard time functioning. The only thing that keeps me going is the lovely ongoing conversation I am having with the voice of my supposed over-active imagination, which is now sending support, "Hang in there, Jody. Trust in the process."

The voice is always loving and kind, but this time I interject negatively with doubt: "Hang in there? I have no clue what I am doing and no clue where I am going! I feel like I am cursed and you're saying hang in there? And, I think I am totally crazy for having a conversation with you in the first place."

Again I am met with loving: "Totally understandable. The world beyond the eyes is camouflaged by the illusion of physical reality. The limbo state you currently encounter is temporary. It's okay that you don't trust. You've been through much that would invite that. You may wish to grant your trust in the near future. For now I remind you of something your heart will remember. Reality is always kinder than our ego makes it seem. With your willingness to let things go that will begin to become clear."

With that I sigh: "I am willing."

I am standing outside my house and suddenly feel completely grounded in the present. All the zoom, zoom, zoom of my mind dissolves. I am still and become aware of the gentle breeze in my hair and the birds chirruping in harmony, their morning ritual. There is a rustle of the wind blowing through the trees that melts my worries away. I feel vibrant and centered, as if nothing else matters. All the fear and self-loathing has come to a halt. And the voice says, "Thank you for your willingness. Out of this will come the many gifts I wish to share and give to you."

I have heard many times that when one aligns with their true calling everything falls into place. Up to this point, in my confused state of mind, I thought that was fluffy gibberish. However, I am beginning to see truth to it. As I stand here in this moment of sweet surrender, the alignment process is in motion. I am reminded it is always darkest before the greatest dawn.

It's been twenty-four hours. I am yet again making my morning ritual walk to the mailbox. Once again I'm filled with anxiety. The only money I have to my name is $660 dollars! And I am holding onto it in case I get accepted to University of Santa Monica. *How am I going to make it? I can't ask my mom for any more help. And no one is responding about a job.*

My mom has been sweet enough to help me out with food and a little gas money to get me from here to Jana's and back. Jana and Larry have been kind and generous as well. But, I don't want it to be like this anymore. I am praying for a miracle.

I open the mailbox filled with worry that this is going to be yet another day with no word from University of Santa Monica. Then, like a magnet, my eyes gravitate to the third envelope down where I see a corner sticking out with the lovely logo of the University of Santa Monica. My stomach drops. *OH MY GOSH! Is it here?! I am so nervous!* My heart begins pounding. I quickly grab it and the rest of the mail, and almost run back to the house.

I bolt through the door: "It's here!"

My mom is startled by my excitement. She swings around from the counter where she is busy fumbling with a white sheet of paper.

"*What's* here? By the way, I have something I want to talk to you about."

She begins to walk toward me with the paper in her hand but I'm unable to focus on it. My excitement about the letter from the University has taken over.

"It's a letter from USM!"

My mom quickly redirects her attention; setting the paper down on the counter. "Oh, cool! Open it."

She is now as focused as I am on the envelope with the beautiful purple logo.

"I'm nervous, Mom."

She gestures to take the envelope from me.

"Want me to open it?"

"No, I'll do it."

In slow motion I tear the top of the envelope off and pull the letter out. The sound of the paper moving seems to echo through the house. My heart is beating so fast and so hard I am surprised it doesn't sound like a drum beat. I begin silently reading the words to myself while my mom waits patiently.

Finally she says, "Well, what does it say?"

I begin to cry. I can't believe it!

"I've been accepted, Mom!!"

With that she flings her arms around me in a big embrace. "I am so happy for you Jod!" Even though I know that she's excited for me, I suspect she is also partially relieved. I think she had a little concern that I wouldn't be accepted and what it would do to my spirit if that had happened.

Knowing I am going to the University in the fall brings about a blended array of feelings. The colors of the bouquet are: excited, nervous, curious, and anxious.

"Oh my Gosh, Mom! I'm really doing this." I'm all lit up! She sees my excitement and smiles and lights up too. I know it touches her heart to see my joy.

But all of a sudden, the logistics begin to sink in. And now worry starts to come across my face. My mom once again chimes in, "It will all work out, Jody. Just keep putting one foot in front of the other."

I am so thankful for her support. Not once has she put any kind of pressure on me by pointing out how irrational it may be to attend a masters program with no job and no money. I lay the rest of the mail down on the counter next to the white paper my mom had just been holding and head to the couch to sit down. She comes over and joins me. We have a lovely hour-long conversation about the University and possible game plans for attending.

It's been about an hour since I've read the acceptance letter. I am standing in my bedroom, stomach full of butterflies, feeling tuned into the hope and possibility of what is to come. There is a part of me that tremendously fears what is transpiring, and then there is a part of me that knows without a doubt this is a blessing.

The very fact that I received confirmation that I am accepted to the USM Masters Program has given me hope that I am not TOO damaged. That is healing in itself. For the first time in a long time I see a light in my life, a direction to head. I know deep inside that this is meant to be and it will all work out somehow.

That is truer than I know. The part I am unconscious of at the moment is that my unseen divine allies, who are as real as you and me, are guiding me. This sense of knowing that it's all going to be okay, is them talking to my heart where the confusion of the ego is non-existent. My soul knows them as family and trusts their wisdom. Our innate inner connection cannot be muffled or skewed by the skepticism of my ego's tendencies.

"Honey?" My mom is knocking on my bedroom door. The butterflies land for a moment on the vine in my mind.

"Come on in, Mom." She walks through the door and sits next to me on my bed. She is once again holding the white paper she set aside earlier when I bolted through the door in excitement.

She is proceeding cautiously as she says, "I wanted to share something with you. I talked to my boss and he feels confident you would qualify for unemployment."

I am agitated by the mere suggestion. My racing thoughts become defensive. *What is she saying? I don't want to go on unemployment. That's for losers. Plus, I quit. I didn't get fired.*

She is picking up on my resistance and says, "I know it's not something you *want* to do but it will be temporary until you find a job. That's what it is for … to help people out of tough situations." I guess she has a point. "Read this sheet. It goes over why you may qualify and how to begin the process if you choose to do so."

I take the sheet from her hand and begin scanning. A part of me recognizes that my prayer for a miracle is being answered right here. I realize that *everything is falling into place.*

CHAPTER 29

Learning to ask for help

My momentary consideration for filing for unemployment is taken over once again by my resistance.

With a heavy sigh, I lower the paper to my lap and scratch my head in distraction. I turn to my mom. Her eyes are gentle and caring. It's as if she knows exactly what I'm thinking, "It's going to be okay," she says.

This seems to be her divine mantra to me these days. Her keen awareness of how hard I am being on myself for my current circumstances seems to welcome such a statement.

"I don't want help from anyone, Mom, including you, or Sammy, or Dad, or Jana and Larry. I am lost, Mom, this is all so much. This is never how I thought my life would end up. I especially don't want help from the government. That would mean I am totally a loser." I look down at the paper, "The last thing I want is a handout from anybody. I never meant to be here."

Her hand reaches out to mine, "Never let life drag you down, Jod. There are times in life where you need to pull yourself up by the bootstraps. This is one of those times. Take each step as it comes." Up until this point, my mom has never suggested I take such a path as the one she is now suggesting.

"I know you feel stuck, shunned, and ashamed, Jody. I know you don't want to receive help of any kind and maybe that's something you should look at. Be gentle on you. We are here for you, your family I mean … Sammy loves you,

Dad loves you, Dani loves you, Jana and Larry love you, we are here to support you through this. And, I don't mean in a financial manner. I know the financial aspect is important to you to figure out on your own. It has been clear from the beginning of your journey of applying to USM that paying for it is something you must do on your own. You'll get a job. Keep at it. In the meantime think about reading this paper over and consider at least applying."

She grabs my hand again, giving it another loving squeeze, and gets up to leave the room.

"Thanks Mom, I love you."

I look down at the paper once again, seriously thinking about what she said. As I read the document it states something to the effect of, "The employee must be out of work through no fault of their own. An interview will determine if that is so."

Handwritten in the corner I see a note from my mom: "You had to quit for your safety."

Wow, that statement is piercing. I sit quietly with my thoughts. Her handwriting in the corner drives right through the burden of guilt and blame. It offers a tiny sliver of possibility that maybe all the mishaps that have happened in my life are not mine to bear on my own. Her support offers light to the irrational belief I am meant to torture myself all the way to my grave. *Maybe she's right. Maybe this is what unemployment is for and maybe I should consider it.*

I look down at her handwriting once again. The letters blare out at me: YOU HAD TO QUIT FOR YOUR SAFETY.

My ego begins to relax enough to consider this, *I did have to quit for my safety … I guess that is a reason outside of my own. I'm sure I won't qualify, but maybe I should give it a try. What could it hurt? I'll speak from my heart and let God do the rest.*

After a few days of mulling over it, I reluctantly send off my application.

CHAPTER 30

Out of denial into divine presence

Today is the day for the unemployment interview.

I am home alone awaiting the phone call. I am pacing back and forth in the kitchen in anticipation.

Why am I so nervous?

I ponder the thought. What I realize is I am already fearful of talking about the details of what happened with Wade to those who are closest to me. So, the thought of sharing it with a *government official* is even more nerve-racking. I begin to nibble on my nails as the minute mark slowly approaches.

With a jolt I hear the *riiiinging* of the phone.

It sure sounds especially loud today. As I answer it, all the shame and blame I am holding down inside begins to bubble to the surface. I say a quick prayer: *Be with me God, I give this to you.*

I answer the phone with a meek "Hello."

The woman on the other end is surprisingly kind. I had pictured all government officials as being insensitive, but she is quite the contrary. We've been talking for a good ten minutes and I am finally finding myself beginning to feel a little more at ease. In the background I wonder, *is she an angel?*

"Did he ever hit you?" Her question pangs my heart.

"He only made physical contact once where he pushed me down the hallway. Other than that he never made physical contact but it was heading in that direction rather quickly. There were countless threats, one of which was when he broke his fist on the granite countertop, yelling at me, telling me he didn't like me very much. He ended up needing a cast."

"Did you ever call the police?"

"No, I wanted to, and even told him I was going to on several occasions, but then became too fearful he would actually follow through. His ex-wife called the cops on him before they divorced … and charges were placed against him. I thought she was making his behavior up, but I now see there was truth to her allegations."

There is a continued exchange between us with her questions and my answers.

"Why did you quit your job?"

"I felt I had to … for my safety. The night before I quit he pulled the covers back at three a.m., threatening me in a way I knew, if I didn't distance myself soon, I could be in serious danger."

A few more questions are asked, each of the same nature. One by one I meet them with heartfelt vulnerability.

"Well Jody, I thank you for your time. You will receive something soon in the mail regarding our decision, and if we have any further questions we'll be in touch."

All of a sudden, and much to my surprise, I blurt out, "What do you believe the outcome will be?"

"Jody, in cases such as domestic abuse we almost always go in favor of approving the case."

That should have been good news! But the words "domestic abuse" hit me like a freight train. We end our call and those words echo loudly through my whole being. *Domestic abuse? Me? No way.*

Alone with those words I sit in silence for the next hour realizing their truth. I am coming out of denial. I am gaining altitude over the last few years and can see clearly the sea of red flags I left behind. *Thank you dear God for always guiding me even when I didn't always know it.* Warmth comes over me as I hear, "I love you. I am always with you."

When the unemployment claim is approved my feelings are bittersweet. But soon I appreciate the benefits. It is giving me enough independence to provide for my own groceries and gas money.

Now I am sitting at my mom's home desk scanning the computer for any possibility of a job that I might have missed. With every passing moment the worries increase: *How am I going to get a job that will support taking one day off per month for school? I have never had a job that supported me that way.*

My heart sinks and for a moment I let go, wanting to give up.

I push myself away from the computer, placing my head in my hands. I let out a heavy sigh of frustration. Somehow, the zooming of my mind quiets enough for me to hear, "Talk to me … turn to me … I promise to help you out of where you are."

I stop in my tracks both inwardly and outwardly. I am half-startled and half-soothed. The energy behind the words is loving and gentle. I release my hands from my head, close my eyes, and take a deep breath. The voice continues, "There you go, Sweet Angel, relax and let go for a moment."

I sit quietly with my hand on my heart in prayerful meditation. The frantic moments I experienced earlier subside as I hear, "Everything is going to be okay. I know it's hard to believe right now. Trust in the inner knowing of your heart."

With each breath, I tune into the deeper levels of my being. I feel my worry turning into inspiration. In this moment, as I sit with my eyes closed, hand to heart in inner communion I know, without a doubt, I am meant to be at USM. I know that everything will continue to fall into place. Even though my ego cannot make sense of it, or make sense of this loving voice within, there is a part of my soul that has unwavering faith. There is a part of me that trusts wholeheartedly what's transpiring. I am filled with warmth and as I go to open my eyes, I hear one last word of encouragement: "Every step of the way I am with you."

Allies & Mentors

CHAPTER 31

Finding the warrior within

"Ready to go?!" My mom's face is bright and cheerful. The first day of class is here and we're about to get on our way! Over the last few months she and I have had several conversations about the logistics of school. She is a saint and has offered to drive down to L.A. once a month on the weekends I have class.

At first I refused, but as she kindly pointed out I am able to use her car while she visits with my sister and her grandchildren who live close to USM. How can I refuse that? We're zooming down the freeway. I watch as the scenery passes by the window in a half daydream, half napping state. The humming of the wheels is mesmerizing as I get lost in thought of what is to come.

"Auntie Jody! Grammy!" We have arrived at my sister's house. My nieces Zoe and Ella are bolting from the front door in a full sprint to greet us. The love from these two is contagious and endearing. "Auntie Jody, I am so happy you are here!" Ella swings her arms around my waist burying her head in my tummy. "Me too!" I hear Zoe from behind me. I am literally sandwiched. "I'm happy I am here too. I've missed you guys."

"Okay, give her some air you two." My sister is gesturing for them to release me from their love pack. She greets me with a long hug. "So glad you're here, Jod."

As the hour approaches to leave for the University, I can feel my energy getting intense. My family and I have been visiting in my sister's living room since we got here. I am nervous and, as the minutes tick by, I am becoming irritable and cranky, so I excuse myself for a second. The only place I can think to take refuge is in the bathroom. I sneak inside for a moment and slowly close the door behind me. I notice my hand is shaking. I close the lid to the toilet seat, sit down, and put my head in my hands. I am fighting back the tears. *God, I don't even know if you're real or if the voice I hear is you. But I need your help. I am really beginning to freak out. I don't know if I can do this. I leave for school in less than an hour and I'm terrified.*

I keep my head firmly held in my hands hoping for some sort of response. Without a second's hesitation the loving consciously connects, "Thank you Sweet Angel for turning to me. I know this is not easy. What you are embarking on is a beautiful journey, not for the faint of heart, but you can do this. Hold your head high in steadfast confidence that you are on the right path. I promise there is beauty transpiring beyond what you are currently able to see. Do as you have always done, which is to follow the stepping stones before you. Trust in your purpose; it is exquisitely radical and powerful. I encourage you to tap into your heart right now and hold onto what it says."

I take a few deep breaths and do just that, tap into my heart.

"What does it say, Sweet Angel?"

"It says there is no doubt and to trust."

"Yes, trust in the truth of what it says. It is not leading you astray. Nor am I ... I love you."

With that I pull my head from my hands and open my eyes.

The bathroom seems brighter, my energy lighter. I feel plugged into the warrior within. *I can do this! I am doing this!* With that I open the bathroom door and walk out with authority, ready to take this USM thing on in full force.

"Okay everyone, see you tonight when I get back. Wish me luck."

There is a chaotic shuffle of goodbye hugs, "I love you!" and "Have fun!" I must look like a deer in the headlights. And with that, out the door I go, terrified.

As the front door shuts, a lovely ocean breeze greets me, taking me back to my prayer from moments ago. I hear the loving words of encouragement once again, "Trust your heart." The memory is just enough to take the edge off of my fear. I keep repeating this mantra as I walk to my mom's car. I fling the door open, plop down and go to start it up. A wave of knowing comes over me. "I encourage you to take a moment to center." I know it's a good idea, so I pause with a deep breath in. I place my hand to my heart, closing my eyes. *Here I go, God, I've jumped!*

CHAPTER 32

A hopeful beginning

The University of Santa Monica is conveniently located about ten miles from my sister's house. I feel lucky my commute to school is not as challenging as it will be for many of my classmates, who come each and every month from all over the country and from other parts of the world.

However, driving in L.A. on two of the main freeways, on a Friday at 5:30 p.m., is not an ideal situation. I'm already anxious about heading to class for the first night. The experience of unknown freeways and unclear directions is nerve-wracking. As I approach the freeway, I see it's bumper-to-bumper traffic just like my sister Samantha said it would be. Thankfully, she gave some great advice on how best to navigate through. Her words are now ringing in my head. "Get the whole way over to the left lane." So, cutting off a few people in the process, that is what I am doing, igniting a chain reaction of car honking in the process. I believe I may have even evoked the birdie from one driver.

I'm finally over to the left lane where it becomes smooth sailing. I let out a sigh and settle in. The drive is quick and before I know it I have arrived at the parking structure of USM. I am definitely feeling like a deer in the headlights now.

I waste no time and hop out of the car and head straight to the USM building. Any more time to think and I may have a panic attack. As I approach the main door of the building I notice a crowd of people standing outside. That is throwing

my butterflies into full flight. I walk to the door with my head
a little low. There is a lovely lady greeting us at the main
entrance. "Hi and welcome. Come on in." I look up to see she
has the face of an angel and the energy of a saint. Her smile is
calming and soothing. I smile back as I walk wide-eyed into
the building of new beginnings.

I am taken by the hustle and bustle of the entourage of
volunteers. Thankfully, not much thinking is required on my
part. Everywhere I turn there is a helpful person supporting
the process of the first night. After thirty-five years of teaching
spiritual psychology, it seems USM is a well-oiled machine.

One of the volunteers catches my eye, "Did you complete
your paperwork?" I feel intimidated by the personal attention.
"Yes. I did," I answer with a sheepish response. The volunteer
meets me with only compassion and love as he gently gestures
up the stairs. "You can head on up to the classroom if you
like." I smile, muttering a thank you.

As I walk up the stairs I am extremely uncomfortable
in my body. My resistance is in full force. I feel ashamed,
insecure, and want to run and hide. It is by sheer willpower
that I am making it to the top of the stairs. With every step I
keep hearing, "Trust your heart."

As I turn to head to the door I am greeted by another two
women whose light is as bright as a beaming sun on a beautiful
day. I believe they sense my vulnerability and gift me with a
smile that speaks volumes. Their loving hold somehow gives
an unspoken invitation to trust that I am meant to be here.

Through the doors of the classroom I go, making a beeline
for a middle seat two rows back from the front of the room.
With a magnetic pull I put my butt in the chair and feel as if
I have just won a marathon. *I made it! I did it! We have lift off!*

The excitement in the room is palpable. Nervous, anxious,
excited, joy-filled … it's all here. Finally, the journey is getting

started. We are gently being asked to quiet down. We're about to hear a formal opening talk from one of the key faculty at USM. The room becomes silent. She has my full attention. She is speaking quite highly of Drs. Ron and Mary Hulnick. I feel impatient for their arrival in the room. Finally she introduces them. "It is my honor to introduce to you Drs. Ron and Mary Hulnick."

There is a loud burst of loving acknowledgement from those who know them. As I look around the room I see many in standing ovation. I notice every single one of them is looking on with pure love. *There it is again. They are literally beaming.* I turn around to see Ron and Mary coming down the center aisle. *Wow, she's beautiful.* Not only is Mary a stunningly gorgeous woman, but also there is something about her energy that has immediately touched my heart.

Until they reach the stage my eyes are stuck to them like glue. Licia, the faculty member who introduced them, is standing at their side. With friendly words of acceptance they take their seats of navigation at front and center. I don't even realize that I'm holding onto my chair with a death grip. I close my eyes in prayer.:

Here we go ... please don't let them take advantage of me the way DJ did. I trust my heart, God.

My inner tone is one of authentic intent, not victimhood. But, I do have fear. Tremendous fear. All of my past is beginning to come to the forefront, temporarily blinding me to the beautiful reality I currently sit in.

But miraculously, as each word is being spoken into the room, my nerves begin to ease. Ron's endearing humor begins to break through my fear. With his candid and touching way, my heart begins to open, as does every heart in the room I sense. Rich moments of laughter break the obvious tension we are all feeling with jumping off this unknown cliff.

Mary's love is tangible, endearing, and heavenly. Her way of being charismatically touches the core. I have never felt such a mixture of feelings. I know I am meant to be here, yet part of me wants to run out the door. I feel a wave of calm, yet my heart is beating loudly with anxiety. I feel an undeniable inner knowing of the authenticity of Drs. Ron and Mary Hulnick, but I am examining every word they say looking for a reason not to trust.

Yet, identical to the grace of wind filling an adventurous sail, this breath of new life is setting course for a magnificent new horizon. I may not know where we are headed, but I sense divine allies, seen and unseen, masterfully guiding the ship.

Before I know it the evening has flown by and I am headed back to my sister's with day one down. It's well past 11:00 p.m. as I get out of the car. It's especially dark with it being a new moon and there's a slight October chill in the air. I pause for a moment taking in a deep breath. *Thank you, God.* There has always been something really special about this time of the year. Something in the air has always moved me to a place deep inside myself, but I have never been able to put my finger on why. Tonight is not any different. I slowly open my sister's front door and hear my mom's voice. I flinch a little not expecting anyone to be awake.

"How was it?"

I've barely made it through the front door before seeing her half-lit silhouette outlined in the dark room. I walk closer to her and see she is now looking like a deer in the headlights. I assume she has been worried.

"It was good! Mostly logistics and outlining what's to come."

Even as I say that, I sense I am not sure anyone can outline with words what really is to come.

"Oh, I am so happy to hear it!" She scans my face to see if

I am in a good zone. She looks extremely relieved. "I'm going to head to bed now." It's way past her bedtime. She is sleepy-eyed as she gives me a hug.

"Thanks for waiting up for me, Mom."

"Sure. I wanted to know how it went. Everyone else is asleep but they were thinking about you too."

The house is still with only the crickets chirping outside. I am a little wound up, so I sit alone with my thoughts in a moment of decompression. My mind scans the evening. Even though the night was mostly about setting the foundation for the course work, something in my soul is stirring deeply. I can sense myself about to stretch experientially into a whole new level of being.

CHAPTER 33

But now the time has come to talk

It's the morning of day two at USM. My alarm is going off way too early. I hit the silence button and slowly pull myself from the bed, knowing I haven't time to go back to sleep. I drowsily walk to the kitchen, rubbing my eyes in an attempt to wake up. I'm in my own space, assuming I am the only one awake this early on a Saturday morning.

"How you doing, Jod? How was last night?"

My sister's voice startles me, but I'm happy to see she is awake. Her sweet smile and warm eyes bless me. I see she is sipping her morning coffee at the kitchen table, busy with something on her computer.

"It was good. Lots of logistics outlining what's to come and what spiritual psychology is."

"Oh cool," she closes her computer giving me her full attention. "Do you remember what they said?"

"Oh gosh I think so ... I believe they said it's something along the lines that we're spiritual beings having a human experience here to learn, grow, and heal."

She beams another smile at me, "So sounds like your cup of tea."

I pour myself a cup of coffee as she gestures for me to join her at the table. I'm grateful for this chance to talk. I'm feeling a little overwhelmed.

"They also said something about discovering who I truly am and my purpose here … "

Having said that, a look of confusion and worry crosses my face. My sister picks up on it, not missing a beat. "This is great, Jod. Ever since I can remember you have been saying you know you are here for a purpose, but you simply can't remember what it is yet. You're in the right place at the right time, it sounds like you are meant to be at USM."

Her support is greatly appreciated. It's helping to lift the confusion and worry a little. "Thanks Sammy, not only am I concerned if I am doing the right thing by attending USM, I am also really concerned about not having a job to pay for it. If something doesn't come up in the next week or so I don't even know if I will be back next month."

"Don't worry about that right now. Remember my friend Cheryl who attended USM? She shared with me sometime back that many people in her class were struggling financially and somehow they made it. Somehow, some way, the money always came in for people. Trust in that Jod. It will all work out."

Her words are very encouraging. I allow myself to receive the inspiration they offer and let go of worry for now.

Before I know it the morning has rolled on and I am back in the USM classroom for Day Two. I am standing in the middle of the classroom somehow aware I've boarded an extraordinary vessel of liberation. I close my eyes, clasping hands with the people next to me in an unbroken chain of prayer. Three hundred people close their eyes in unity. As I listen to the words of blessing the energy brings a tremble to my body, escorting my awareness to the tangible presence of Spirit in the room. In my mind's eye, I am reaching to touch the Divine. I stand in symbolic splendor, brushing my soul against a soft petal of exquisiteness blessing me with the fragrance of purpose beyond words.

The prayer creates a sacred space where a pin drop could echo. We continue to stand hand in hand as she gracefully finishes with, "May it be so," and with that, I slowly open my eyes. The room is bright. I feel enlivened and centered. Each person at my side gives a gentle loving squeeze to my hand. I squeeze back in acknowledgement. We take our seats in unintended unison, sending a slight reverberation through the stillness of the air. We shut our eyes for a five-minute peace meditation. The loving energy of Spirit pours into me effortlessly. I send it forth and say a prayer in silence: "I can feel you God. And, I can feel where we are headed. I am willing, even though I am scared, I am willing."

The familiar warmth comes over my body. "Thank you Sweet Angel. I am with you, every step of the way. Thank you for your willingness. It's paves a gracious path to new life."

I sit in silence, a slight tear misting the corner of my eye. Even with the comfort of the words I hear I know full well at some point I will be sharing my past heartache with another. That thought is terrifying.

"Good Morning!" Ron's enthusiasm is contagious. There is a twinkle in his eye that says *this is going to be fun.* He is sitting at center stage with Dr. Mary Hulnick and Licia at his side. The words their lips impart catch the attention of my heart. Ron reiterates part of yesterday's content, "As we mentioned last night, spiritual psychology is the study and practice of the art and science of human evolution in consciousness."

I scrunch my eyebrows in confusion. *What does that mean?*

As if he knows exactly where I am, Ron adds, "Some of you may wonder *what exactly does that mean?* Put another way, spiritual psychology is a technology that empowers students to convert their everyday life experience into rungs on the ladder of spiritual evolution. This educational process results in students experiencing greater connection to who they are, their life's purpose, and enhanced levels of success and fulfillment. This empowers them to make a meaningful contribution in their world."

I feel Spirit tugging on my heart chord to pay attention. Yet, the fearful part of me takes the lead, deafening me to what I hear. I'm afraid the wrath of DJ is sure to come around.

Out of the floodgates we go. The morning is rockin' and rollin'. As I listen to Ron and Mary speak, the death grip on my seat becomes tighter and tighter. My paranoid ego has me engaged in thinking what I hear is going to take me down the same powerless road I went with DJ. I am paralyzed by the reflection of my past, which casts a shadow of irrational assumptions that my power will be used for shady ego-based purposes as it was with DJ.

But deep down I realize that nothing could be further from the truth. There is a higher part of me that stands beyond fear, recognizing that this is about authentic empowerment. Ron and Mary's devotion to ushering in light and love to this earth as a "we" thing is clear as day to my soul. It can see they are not domineering "gurus" such as DJ, claiming to know the only truth, but "Wayshowers" of the light, giving sight to the truth that we are all beings of love on the road to awakening.

The morning has been a steady flow of brilliant insight. We're beginning to learn "soul-centered basic skills," which are at the core of Spiritual Psychology. The first two we are being introduced to are "Seeing the Loving Essence" and "Heart-Centered Listening." As I listen to the powerful foundation of each I feel liberated! Seeing the Loving Essence is about seeing others and yourself through the eyes of Loving. It is the essence of the Buddhist greeting, Namasté, which is a conscious recognition that the soul within me recognizes the soul within you. Heart-Centered Listening means opening our spiritual hearts with genuine care, and listening on all levels of our being to the content, tonality, and meanings of what another is saying while tuning into the energy the message is riding upon with authenticity. It's a true art indeed.

Yet, as lovely as the skills are intellectually, I find myself in a panic when we are informed that we will be practicing each of the skills in an experiential manner through what is called a Trio. My biggest fear is coming true! I'm going to be talking to another about what has happened and sharing vulnerably!

But thankfully, I will soon come to realize our time spent in trios is a miraculous gift. It is about choice, and by choosing the road of courage and going inward for healing and transformation the course of my life will be altered in a profound way.

The trios are harbor for the ship to come home. They consist of three people sitting in a triangular seating arrangement. One person is the client, another is the facilitator, and the third person is the silent observer. The client and facilitator sit face to face, while the silent observer is to the left of the facilitator and to the right of the client. In every trio we will rotate seats to experience each of the chairs. Every trio has guidelines for what is to be covered and reviewed before we start. They are designed to deepen the mastery of the skill we have just learned. In this case, the trio is about Seeing the Loving Essence and Heart-Centered Listening.

The love from the volunteer staff is impeccable. They are here to support and assist us with how to do this and when to switch spots. Even so, in this moment, the thought of actually participating in a trio is terrifying to me.

I look over at Dr. Ron Hulnick as he utters what I feel is going to lead me to my doom. I watch as his mouth seems to be moving in slow motion with the words pouring out in slow motion: "Please turn your chairs into standard trio format." The words echo through the room bouncing off all

297 students.

The anxiety I feel must be commonplace, for Ron is keeping it light with his lovely humor. I look at him again and see that same twinkle in his eyes that tells us, *this is going to be fun.* He addresses the class with his vibrant voice:

"The good news is, turning your chairs into standard trio format seems to be the hardest part for all the USM students who have attended."

He is poking fun at the fact that we're having a little bit of difficulty navigating the chairs into the allotted threesome structure. There are people bumping into one another. The room has a low rustle from the movement of accidental interlocking of chairs. I hear a murmur of "Sorry ... excuse me," followed by giggles of discomfort, which are a welcome distraction. Once we are settled in, we close our eyes and center. Mary, with her angelic voice, guides us though a lovely centering process. I say a silent prayer: *Here I go God. Be with me.*

CHAPTER 34

The miracle of immediate intimacy

I sit with my eyes closed, mentally preparing to face my fear of talking to another person about my personal life.

My mind wanders, much like on a dreamy lazy day where I meet the loving within. "I love you Sweet Angel. Your prayers are always heard and answered. I am with you. Thank you for your courage."

As I sit here in a half-altered state I am beginning to think this voice within is not simply a figment of my over-active imagination, but much more a direct channel to the Divine. I cannot deny the knowingness that comes over me when we speak, and even though I am still unsure, much to my blessed surprise, over the next two years I will discover the truth.

With that, my attention is drawn back into the classroom where it's being announced that we are to start our first trio: "When you are ready you may please begin." My stomach drops.

I slowly open my eyes and sitting before me is a lovely woman. I think, thank goodness I am in the "facilitator chair" first, because I'm already worried about what I'm going to say once I am in the client chair. I'm doing my best to redirect my nervousness. *Am I messing this up? What am I going to say when I'm in the client chair? Does this person think I am weird?* Round and round my thoughts go.

My hands are clutching the handouts that are sitting in my lap. I am nervously fumbling around with them, trying to avoid showing my embarrassment and nervousness. Luckily for me, I sense my trio mates are as nervous as I am. We're in this together, and to my surprise something very magical is beginning to happen. With each passing moment my thoughts begin to calm down, allowing a new awareness to arise. In the woman before me I see a glow. My listening is deepening in a way I have never experienced, taking on a new perspective. I begin to hear what she is saying, but not from merely a verbal standpoint. On the wings of intuition I am receiving the message of her heart. She senses the openness, and it deepens her courage to authentically express herself in our conversation. Her vulnerability is inspiring. She is misty around her eyes as she shares a little of what brought her here to USM. Time becomes absent and before we know it, *ding!* Our time is up. She looks as shocked as I do. "What, is that it?"

I respond in kind: "I know … how is that possible?"

We are given five minutes for feedback. The precious soul before me begins gifting me with her kind acknowledgements. Being a master deflector I do not know what to do with them.

She says, "Jody, thank you. I could feel your love and support. I was really nervous about doing this and you created a space for me to open up. I felt heard and loved."

I am touched by her kind words and relieved to know I am not the only one who is nervous. I feel an intimacy with her that is unexplainable and beautiful. In the remaining time we have left, the three of us continue to share what we experienced. With each heartfelt word my heart begins to open more and more. Soon, though, my moments of calm are turned around. We are being prompted to rotate our seating. It's my turn in the hot seat! I am in a sea of anxiety as we briefly center again before the second round begins. I am almost deafened by the loud beating of my heart.

Holy crap. I can't do this!

Without a moment of hesitation my friend from within speaks again: "Breathe, Sweet Angel. You're going to be okay. Speak from your heart and all else will follow. Your willingness is all it takes … it's enough."

I am beyond thankful for the encouragement, for in this moment I am beside myself with fear. The supportive words calm the thumping in my chest allowing a wave of courage to come through. I feel an air of acceptance as I manage to whisper, "Thank you" before popping my eyes open to face the gentleman sitting before me in the facilitator chair.

Miraculously, speaking from my heart is exactly what I begin to do. I say it as it is, and with every honest heartfelt word healing transpires: "I'm really nervous about being here and talking to you. I've been through so much and not sure what to do about it."

I am looking directly into my facilitator's eyes. All I see is love in return. I begin to tear up.

He says, "I hear you and hear what you're saying. I completely understand. I am right here with you."

His gentleness creates the space for me to fully open up. I share with him a bit about what brought me here to USM and a little of my past. With each passing minute I surprisingly find myself going deeper into what I am sharing. *Ding!* Again, the bell for completion comes quickly. That wasn't so bad! I am smiling a smile I thought I had lost some years ago. I feel a sense of freedom that I have never felt before. I notice I am energetically lighter. And I'm amazed at how close I feel to my trio mates. We all speak of how truly miraculous it is to feel this close to each other when we technically just met.

Seeing the Loving Essence and Heart-Centered Listening naturally opens the door to authentic intimacy. As we bring our trio to completion I am keenly aware the journey of transformational awakening has begun.

CHAPTER 35

The beginning of self-forgiveness

"Out beyond ideas of wrongdoing and rightdoing there is a field. I'll meet you there."
~ *Rumi*

We are given a little time to write in our journal any notes we wish to take from the trio process we have just completed. There is lovely music humming in the background, nurturing the peaceful feeling I have. I keep thinking to myself, *all that worry and that wasn't so hard.*

I begin to see how fear gets in the way of new possibility. The music fades to an end and we are asked to bring our notes to completion. I close my journal to look up and see Ron and Mary back at center stage. Journals are rustling to a close as people adjust to get comfortable in their chairs. The group attentiveness is palpable. Once everyone is settled and focused, Ron begins.

"Okay, so how was that?" he asks. "We'll take a little sharing from the process. Raise your hand and, once you're called on, please stand up and we'll bring you a microphone. Make sure to start with your name."

Ron's invitation ignites butterflies in my stomach. *There is NO WAY I'll ever share in the front of the class.* The loud voice of my ego is convincing, making that seem a certainty. Yet, my playing small is not quite what Spirit has in mind. What I don't foresee is that in the not-so-far-off future I will be sharing with all 300 hundred people in this room how the incredible healing process we are currently undertaking has opened a door to a profound change and a great love—I will soon be sharing I've met the man I will marry.

Through what I experience I will see all of what transpires in our lives is always *for us.* Even my "horrific" past was not a mistake. It is ultimately what shaped and created the foundation for growth to take place. It has removed the stagnation of a wayward path, taking with it clay that was not the gem of my soul. In due time, I will be standing to share this with the class.

But for now I simply watch as Mary scans the hands of those brave souls who are willing to take a vulnerable risk. It's as if she can sense where the energy of Spirit is for the highest good. With a sudden flash I remember when I first considered USM. I was sure, without a doubt, that the people who facilitated it would be living in the land of hippy-dippy.

Nothing could be further from the truth.

Not only is USM infused with an air of professionalism that meets the standard of any highly accredited academic institution, USM is also infused with grace. It is quite extraordinary to experience.

Mary stops and gestures to one of my female classmates sitting across the room:

"Okay Sarah ... please, we'll start with you." Mary's smile is bright and inviting. I sense an air of peace from her that is calming to my soul.

My classmate, Sarah, slowly comes to her feet and takes the microphone from one of the assistants. She places her hand to her heart and takes in a deep breath. She lowers her head for a moment before proceeding in an attempt to compose herself. She is obviously nervous and, to me, rightfully so. Mary gently guides her to begin: "Please start with your name."

"Hi, I'm Sarah."

She pauses taking in another breath. We all feel her fear and willingness to be vulnerable. It is courageous and inspiring.

"I am very grateful to be here, and a little scared to be standing up and sharing but what I just experienced was so amazing." She pauses for a moment. "It's been quite a journey getting to USM ... I faced so much resistance both inwardly and outwardly."

She pauses again to look around the room, not realizing how profound her last statement is. What is within is truly without.

"One of my key resistances to coming here was I believed nobody would understand ... I really thought what I've been through was too much and that I was too damaged. I thought nobody would care, or nobody would hear me, or get me."

Her face lights up. "What I just experienced proves that is not so! I don't think I have ever been heard before now. My facilitator was authentic and present with me. I don't know how to explain other than I *know* he understood me ... I know he genuinely wanted to be here for me and listen with his whole heart. I felt his love."

Tears begin to well up in her eyes, as they do in mine. There is another moment of pause before Sarah proceeds with sharing in more detail what brought her here to USM. The events in her life are of tragedy and despair, which touch me to the core. I can certainly relate, given the nature of my own past. I find myself relieved to hear I am not the only one who has been hit by a spiritual two-by-four!

Mary works with Sarah for quite some time, never wavering in her loving intent to be with Sarah. Her intention is as clear as the North Star on the evening of a new moon. She holds a safe space for her, as we all do, as she expresses her heartache and her hurt. Sarah gracefully comes to a place where the hurt comes up. She places her hands to her face with tears streaming down her cheek. Mary continues to gently meet her where she is: "Sarah, it's okay to let that come up."

The silence in the room is palpable, filled with the timelessness of love. We continue holding a space for her as she begins to let it all go. She finally removes herself from hiding behind her hands, meeting Mary eye to eye, "If only I could do this."

Mary meets her with compassion. "If you could only what, Sarah?" The invitation takes Sarah deeper.

"Be done with all this," Sarah says, "my past, the hurt … all of it! I want freedom. That's why I am here."

Sarah's commitment to "being done" is obvious. I feel her words as if they were my own.

Mary says, "I acknowledge you for your courage in bringing this forward. It is of great service to you as well as to all of us. I hear you and what you are saying about the trying times of your life. I can appreciate how hard they have been. I acknowledge your tremendous strength of heart in standing here now. Your bravery is admirable. In the face of adversity you have stood true to who you are. Your self-honoring choice has a very profound impact, Sarah."

Sarah's energy begins to lighten as she listens and responds, "I just don't know the way through all that has happened. It's a heavy load. And, I don't even know why I brought this all up. I wasn't expecting this."

"Well, I am so thankful you did," Mary says, "Where we are going next is tailor-made for what you have brought forward. It's a soul-centered skill called Compassionate Self-Forgiveness."

Compassionate what? I think to myself. As confused as I may be right now, I will soon realize this is a key to my own liberation.

Mary continues, "As the primary foundation of spiritual psychology it provides a gateway to the truth of who we are."

Sarah looks confused. "Forgiveness of ourselves? This doesn't make sense to me. If we want to forgive, why wouldn't we just forgive the other person?"

Ron now speaks up, "Mary may I add something here?"

Mary gestures yes by way of a nod. The two of them are an excellent team. Ron pops up from his chair heading to a wooden stand sitting on the side on the stage. It is holding a large, blank flip chart.

"See, let's try this out from another angle. As you may remember from yesterday, we mentioned here at USM we talk about two very different and unique contexts."

He is now drawing a line horizontally at the bottom of the page with an arrow at each end of the line. At the left end of the line there is a negative sign and the right side there is a positive sign. He is labeling this line as the *Goal Line.*

"This is the Goal Line of life. This is how we relate with our world—things like our jobs, our relationships, our health—it's those things we would like to have go from 'not as good' to 'as great as it can be.' Most of us have been brought up in this context, and brought up to believe this is the only context that our experience operates in. We all want to be as financially successful as possible, have the best possible relationships … you get the idea. The Goal Line is only one context."

Sarah's wheels begin to stir, as do mine.

"Is this clear for you so far?" He gestures to Sarah.

"Yes, so far it's absolutely clear. Just a little confused on how this relates to self-forgiveness, or even what that is."

Ron smiles with an ever-endearing twinkle present in his eye. His passion for spiritual psychology is incredibly inspiring. "Hang in with me … we're getting there. This lays a great foundation for where we are headed and what you have brought forward."

He gives a moment of pause before continuing.

"The other context is going on simultaneously and we refer to it as the *Learning Line of life.*"

He is now drawing a line vertically down from the top of the page connecting it smack dab in the middle of the Goal Line. The line has an arrow at the top pointing upward. My curiosity is now piqued. I have never heard of such a thing.

"The Learning Line is about how we are *going to be inside of ourselves* as we go along life's path on the Goal Line."

With furrowed brow I try to grasp exactly what it is he is suggesting. There is something to what he says that resonates deeply, yet I know I have never heard anything like this before.

"The Learning Line of life is what we refer to here as Spiritual Evolution."

Ron has now labeled the left of the vertical line as *"spiritual evolution."*

NOW he's speaking my language.

"This is the line when we start to become aware of ourselves as DIVINE BEINGS who are having a human experience— NOT human beings with souls, but rather Divine Beings who are having a human experience."

I can feel the energy of the room attentive and aligned with his flow.

"Here we are in these funny looking bodies doing all kinds of crazy stuff."

There is a giggle in unison rolling through the room. He continues with profound clarity.

"Now the question of all this is why?"

I'm thinking to myself, "exactly!"

"The Goal Line is about success in the world. As much as one might like to obtain total fulfillment on the Goal Line alone, that is not possible. The Learning Line is where the spiritual hunger, spiritual yearning, is fulfilled. This longing is not just in some of us, it's in all of us. It's just some of us are more aware of it than others. It's about answering the question *who am I?"*

I am captivated by the content of the material being presented, as is Sarah, guessing by the change in her posture.

"Are you still with me?"

Sarah nods her head yes. Ron continues without missing a beat.

"It's also about answering the question: What am I doing here? What is my purpose?"

The lights in my mind are flashing off in inspiration. I want to know more! These questions have plagued my heart ever since I can remember.

"We can have purpose on the Goal Line. Some people know what they were born to do, some people were born to be a musician, artist, or singer. Everybody's purpose, while they are here, is growing in spiritual evolution. How do we know if we are growing in spiritual evolution? How do we know if we are evolving spiritually? It's in the loving. We find in every major religion loving is its basic tenet."

Ron has now labeled the very top of the chart with the word LOVING.

"The basic foundation is we become more and more loving people, loving individuals, kind, compassionate, peaceful ... things of that nature. The more we grow spiritually the more our life contains those qualities. You could say we live into them. We live into the loving."

His suggestion puts into motion an invitation toward expanding the limited mindset I have been harboring.

"It's not that we become more loving ... it's that we become more *aware* of our nature as loving beings. Nobody can be more loving, for we are love. Yet we can behave in more loving ways, we can behave in ways that more accurately represent the loving nature of who we truly are. No major religion would quarrel with that statement. We understand this here at USM, that's why we call it Spiritual Psychology. It's a psychology that not only assists people along the Goal Line of life, but more importantly assists people by providing a technology to navigate up the dimension of spiritual evolution, which is our purpose. One powerful key to the technology is Compassionate Self-Forgiveness. What you have shared about your past beautifully articulates what we call the stackers."

Sarah giggles, "If stackers are what I think they, I've had many of them."

The room giggles again as Ron smiles with recognition. He is now slowly drawing a line horizontally back and forth from the positive side of the chart to the negative side of the chart.

"See, we are all here for spiritual evolution whether we are aware of it or not." He is pointing to the Learning Line of life. "Earth is a big school and each of us comes in with a *unique* earth school curriculum."

He points to the Learning Line with clear intent in emphasizing the uniqueness of each of our journeys. "We are here to heal, learn, and evolve. When we get off track, either in suffering in the negative ... " his pen mark is on the negative side of the chart.

" ... or in suffering with the positive."

He pauses as if he heard the confusion in our heads.

"Believe it or not there are many people suffering from too much abundance."

I follow his pen flow over to the positive side. I think to myself, *Well that's interesting. How in the world could too much abundance be a burden?* I let the thought go and quickly return my attention to what's happening in the room.

"Some people do this ... " He is drawing a long stride line

from side to side, crossing over the Learning Line exaggerating being way off course. "We are all here to evolve, to go *up* the Learning Line of life, to awaken into the awareness we are Love and nothing else. This ... " He is pointing to the exaggerated lines he just made. "When this happens, when we get off course, we get feedback from the universe. As in your case, you felt depression, heartache, anger, and hopelessness from the betrayal you perceived you experienced. Would you say this is accurate Sarah?"

Sarah says, "YES absolutely, and I still feel that way."

"Your *upset* is feedback for you that you are off course, you're no longer on the course of the Learning Line. No big deal and nothing *wrong* with it. It's part of our humanness and our journey. Your situation, your experience, what we call your spiritual curriculum, was brought to you by what we conceptually call the Stackers."

There he goes again with those stackers? What the heck is that? My curiosity is in full swing.

"The stackers are our spiritual allies that have no concern with earthly reality. They know all of earth is a school with the purpose of healing and evolution. Their job is to bring in events that are similar to events of our past because they know that those events will serve to bring material forward for healing, which assists us in our spiritual growth. Are you still with me?"

Sarah says, "Yes, I am, and I think I may have many of these stacker things." The entire class bursts into laughter. Both Ron and Mary are chuckling too. Ron continues.

"You mentioned a time when you grew up where you felt betrayed by your mother. You mentioned you internalized it as her not being a great mom ... as her being unloving toward you and abandoning you. Is that accurate?"

Sarah is nodding her head yes.

"This internalization is called a negative judgment, and these judgments interfere with our awareness of being love. Again, there is nothing wrong with this. It's where we are in the evolution of consciousness. From that experience as a child you have placed judgment in your consciousness that has to do with betrayal, not being loved, and abandonment. So, growing up, you took what was present in your consciousness and started translating it into reality as you grew into each successive age level. Make sense?"

Sarah brings the mic back to her chin to answer his question, "So far, yes."

"Great, so what you would find is that periodically people showed up in your life—sometimes spaced apart, sometimes close together, sometimes more than one at a time—where you perceived them as betraying you, not loving you, abandoning you. You've shared a little about this, mentioning relationships and friendships where there have been these elements."

Ron pauses giving time for the information to settle. Then he says, "In their perception they may or may not be doing that. But you define them as doing so, as being that way, and you judged them. This matches the dynamic you internalized in consciousness back then. This is the spiritual opportunity, once you understand the dynamic. This is why the spiritual context, the Learning Line of life, is so important. From this context you start looking at the things that show up in your life on the earthly plane of reality as blessings rather than curses."

My wheels screech to a halt turning in a completely different direction. My ego is triggered, screaming loud thoughts to match: *Blessings? How is what happened with DJ a blessing?* Right on cue my concerns are addressed.

"What may seem like stumbling blocks—such as negative people, your mom, or the fact that she left you and your dad and didn't speak to you for years—from a spiritual point of view, are not. Again, this is why the spiritual context is very important, as is the willingness to take responsibility and release the victim. From the spiritual view, these experiences are actually blessings because they provide the opportunity to face whatever judgments are inside your consciousness that hold you from the realization of who you truly are ... which is a being of Love. Without these experiences with people, or situations, the material would not be triggered to come up for healing. It would lay dormant under the surface of conscious thought. It cannot be healed until it comes up. The Stackers bring us what will best serve us to heal in our evolution. This is where Compassionate Self-Forgiveness comes in. It is a powerful technology for healing and aligning us with the Learning Line of life. By forgiving the negative judgments we have placed on ourselves and the judgments we've placed on others we evolve, awakening us to the truth that we are Spiritual Beings. To remember we are Love. That's why we say in spiritual reality there are no mistakes. There aren't people who shouldn't be here, or events that shouldn't have happened. There's nothing other than repeated opportunity for resolution of unresolved issues."

I break my gaze from Ron for a second, turning to Sarah. I see that she is disturbed. What I see is a mirror reflection of my own inner reality. As I am sitting here witnessing the entire conversation I am having a hard time getting past the whole comment of *be willing to take responsibility and release the victim*. To my surprise Sarah's next words convey that she's right there with me. There is tension in her stance as she shares what's present for her:

"You know, I was following everything you said and was right there with you until you made the comment *be willing to take responsibility and release the victim*. What happened to me is not my fault!"

Her tone is piercing. Mary gestures to Ron, requesting to share something that has come to her. His hand gently invites her to take the reins.

"Sarah, I am so thankful you have brought this up. There is brilliant distinction to be made here that may shed some light on this for you. When we say *be willing to take responsibility and release the victim* we are in no way suggesting you feel guilty, or shameful, or blame yourself for the triggering of hurtful events that have happened in your life that have caused you upset. By taking responsibility we do not mean it is your fault, and, in no way do we condone what has happened to you. What we refer to is outside right and wrong. What we mean by taking responsibility is being willing to take ownership over our reactions, owning the ability we each have to choose our response in any given situation. In taking *response-ability*, we have the ability to choose our response. By doing so we begin to slow down the accumulation of false negative judgment's that keep us bound to suffering in the earthly plane of reality. Once we are willing to take responsibility, to make choices rather than having knee-jerk reactions which land us in the victim world, the door is opened to healing and Spiritual Evolution. Many people, innocently so, are determined from an ego standpoint to be right even if it means being dead right. That is the world of the victim, the world we are encouraging you to let go of. By doing so liberation greets you."

Wow, I am not sure exactly what Mary is saying, but I feel the empowerment behind her words: "You see, the issue is not the issue. The issue is how we relate to ourselves while we go through the issue."

Okay, what did she just say? Now my mind is blown. I keep repeating to myself *the issue is not the issue, it is how we relate to ourselves as we go through the issue … the issue is not the issue, it is how we relate to ourselves as we go through the issue.*

What does that mean? My mind and ego can't grasp it yet. I see Sarah's mind is blown too. She has lowered the microphone to her side, placing her hand to her head. After a few moments she raises the microphone back to her chin and proceeds. "Now you've lost me Mary."

"That's quite alright. This is a very new concept for most and can be challenging to grasp at first. May I use the example of your mom?"

"Sure. Please do."

"With the case of your mom leaving, the issue isn't in her leaving, as hard as that was. The issue is how you were inside yourself when she left. In other words, the issue is all the negative judgments you placed on yourself and on her."

The lights begin to go on in my mind. This is beginning to make sense. Sarah's energy shows signs of clarity beginning to surface as well.

"Ah, I see ... this is beginning to make some sense. But I guess, I'm a little confused about judgments and unresolved issues."

There is a long pause of silence as Sarah continues gathering her thoughts.

"What is present in regard to that, Sarah?"

"Well, how is it that my judgments of the other person are wrong and not the actions of the other? How is it that my mom is not at fault for the heartache she caused me when she left? Why do I need to take responsibility for this?"

"Well, I encourage you to allow for the possibility that your judgments are not wrong, they simply are not the truth of who you are, and they keep you out of alignment to the true nature of your soul, which is love."

Mary smiles at Sarah and then looks at Ron who says, "See, it's not that we are saying your mom doesn't have any responsibility in this. She has *her* curriculum with the experience as well. What we are proposing is that in YOUR taking responsibility for your actions the endless cycle of suffering can begin to heal and be resolved for the last time. The victim perpetuates the suffering of your life … this is true for all of us. Again, we are in no way saying we condone what has happened. We're simply saying in the spiritual context there is a purpose to it, and that purpose is in your healing of unresolved issues."

Sarah wants to hold onto to her righteous position, and I can identify with that. I sure know that I want to blame DJ for everything, and blame Wade for everything too.

She says, "I don't understand how that's possible."

Ron says, "As we mentioned a little while ago, Compassionate Self-Forgiveness is a powerful skill that heals by releasing the false negative judgments and misinterpretations of reality we have placed on our self and others."

Sarah begins to soften: "I think I get what you are saying … and I'm *willing* to let go of the victim … as I said before I really am ready to be done with this … I guess I wonder how do I forgive myself?"

"Great question, and after we get back from the break we'll be going over the soul-centered skill of Compassionate Self-Forgiveness more thoroughly."

There is a long pause as I sense Sarah has arrived at a safe harbor. Mary chimes in with a grounding check-in, "Does all that we have shared give you some direction, Sarah? You really are beautifully set up for the next trio. Are you okay with holding this for a little while?"

Sarah seems light and centered, "This has been amazing … very unexpected and very helpful, but amazing. I am okay with holding where I am. Thank you both."

As Sarah sits down we all applaud in acknowledgement of her courage to share. As she sits down, Ron continues to address the room.

"Before we go on a break I would like to share a little more about unresolved issues. As Sarah asked earlier, 'What is an unresolved issue?' Well, it's ANYTHING that disturbs your peace. And I mean ANYTHING regardless of how justified you may think it is." There are giggles rolling through the room as if people's minds just popped off in memory. "That's right, *even* that one. So, as we mentioned, the conceptualized stackers are the ones whose job it is to make sure we continually get those kinds of experiences so we can continually have the opportunity to heal the issue for the last time. That is the purpose of the earth school curriculum ... To heal unresolved material so we may remember who we are and live in accordance with our true nature as a beings of Love."

The stillness in the room is breathtaking. Inspiration is stirring.

"It's important for us to state that we in no way claim to know the ultimate truth. We encourage you to test all this out for yourself. All we know is what has worked for thousands of students over the last thirty-five years. We invite you to run an experiment and see what works. Take what works and apply it to your own life. Alright ... let's go on a break."

CHAPTER 36

And the new journey begins

As I leave the classroom for the break I find myself immensely grateful to Ron and Mary for acknowledging they do not propose to know the ultimate truth.

Their words give me room to breathe. I can finally begin to separate myself from the fearful memories of my past where I allowed myself to be misled by DJ's assertion that his way was the only way.

As I walk out the classroom door I find myself inspired with new insight and possibility. The coastal breeze passes by over my cheeks, heightening the sense of my ego loosening its guarded grip around my heart. The certainty that I am doomed to this life of suffering is beginning to sway. The expansive insights of the morning have opened a door and are percolating in my mind: *What is this Spiritual Context they speak of? And the stackers? Well, DJ and Wade were definitely stackers!*

There is a glimmer of hope; a beginning of understanding that what transpired in my past had a purpose. I think about what Ron mentioned in regard to the victim within. I reminisce about my intention to take the conscious path of remaining out of that mindset. If anything, I went the other route of total responsibility and self-blame, but there were war wounds I could not deny. I now see that holding all the pain in and taking the path of self-blame and guilt is ultimately another form of being a victim. *Is it possible that all that has happened has been for my growth and evolution?*

I sit on a ledge outside the school building, which seems to have been built just for this purpose, daydreaming about the events of the morning. I am not in much of a socializing mood so I am taking a little time alone. The day is stunningly beautiful. The sun is electric in the bright blue sky with the warm California sun kissing my skin. I close my eyes and listen to the wind rustle through the few trees to my right. There is an inner dance going on with divine awareness. I continue to ponder what has been said, bouncing it off my past difficulties with DJ and Wade. In both instances I perceived betrayal and devastation. Is it *really* possible there is purpose to the madness of dysfunction?

My mind remains dreamy as I reflect on how I have gotten through those challenging times. Had it not been for the enlightened conversations I've had with something greater than myself I am not sure where I would be. I recall the countless occasions I have felt the loving within encouraging me to forgive myself. The suggestion didn't land, for the ground was not yet fertile for the seed. But here I am now, wondering about this thing they call Compassionate Self-Forgiveness. How does this all tie into the nature of healing and evolution? For the first time in my life, I am beginning to consciously experience the spiritual context of reality. For the first time in my life, I have a reference point for what loving is and what forgiveness is and how they tie together.

Soon I am startled out of my meditative state by an assistant walking by with a sign reading "Five Minutes," which she also says out loud. I open my eyes to a whole new world. As I walk back into the classroom I am greeted with a loving hug from one of my classmates, Eliza.

"Wow, what happened to you?" she says. "You're glowing, Jody."

I give her a huge smile. "Eliza, it seems I am guided by an amazing loving energy. I thought it was a figment of my imagination for years and now I realize it is not. I have been blessed with insight about forgiveness that has opened my heart to the possibility of healing."

Eliza begins to get tears.

"I feel you Jody, and it's beautiful."

And, so it begins: The journey of deep healing through forgiveness that will open doors to a life of blessings and miracles.

CHAPTER 37

My future husband finds a coach

Y ou'll remember that we started this book with a wedding scene, the happiest day of my life. The man I married that day (and am happily married to today) is John Vehr.

Now let me pause with my journey at USM, to describe a remarkable experience that had a huge impact on my life, even though I didn't know it was happening at the time. This story I am about to to tell happened while I was at USM:

It begins with two men meeting at a car wash. Seems a simple enough occurrence, right? But yet without the meeting of John Vehr and Blake Hardison there would most likely never be a John and Jody. As you will see, when we are willing to listen within, the Universe masters the process of divine orchestration.

It is the night before John and Blake are to meet, Blake and his wife, Maryn, are having movie night watching Will Smith in *The Pursuit of Happyness* (yes, that's the correct spelling, you have to see the movie for an explanation!). Scenes from the movie are igniting Blake's playfulness, a key factor in the next day's coincidental meeting.

John, on the other hand, has recently returned home from Miami after following a gut feeling to walk away from a situation he thought he was going to stay in. His mood is not good. It's a beautiful sunny Saturday afternoon in March of 2011.

Blake and Maryn have decided to take both their cars to the local car wash. Blake finishes his car first and pulls out of the drive-thru with his playful side in full gear. Maryn, who is directly behind him, is smiling in recognition of her love for him, somehow knowing what he's up to. She temporarily goes her own way to vacuum out her car. Blake slows down to scan the scene. "Hmmm, now let's see … " He is recalling a scene from last night's movie where Will Smith sees a guy with a Ferrari, and says something along the lines of, "Man, what is it that you do, and how can I learn to do that? How can I get me some of *that?*"

Blake being Blake, with his vivacious nature, wants an opportunity to use that line on someone. He glances over the vacant vacuum slots looking for an ideal candidate. The first empty slot is next to a beat up Honda Civic. Blake chuckles. "Nope, that won't work."

He looks a little further down, spotting an opening next to a Porsche Panamera. "Bingo! Now we're talking. Perfect!"

Without hesitation, Blake zips his little black BMW into the slot next to John Vehr who has just gotten out of his brand new pristine black on black Porsche. Blake jumps out, meeting John eye-to-eye from a distance.

"Hey!" He nods toward John, "Nice car!"

John appreciates the acknowledgement, "Thanks man," then goes back about his business not knowing Blake intends to play on.

"Man, what is it that you do, and how can I learn to do that? How can I get me some of that?"

Blake smiles, knowing he has successfully landed the line. He's trying to have fun with John, who is still in a rather low mental state due to the life stuff he has going on. But John turns around giving Blake a smile. He thinks, "Who is this punk kid?" John can't help but begin to snap out of his funk.

Blake's playful energy is delightful and quite infectious.

As they whirl about, having as much fun as two people can while cleaning their cars, they effortlessly share small talk about their lives, about what they do, and who they are. With John being John, and Blake being Blake, the conversation quickly goes a little deeper. Blake recognizes that there is something special about this man.

John is finished with his car and ready to leave.

"Okay, man ... it was good to meet you," John gestures a goodbye while opening his car door to get in. He has one foot on the floorboard when Blake says, "Wait, let me give you something before you go."

John rises back out of his car watching as Blake pops opens his trunk. He heads a little closer to see him fetching something out. He assumes Blake wants to give him a business card like all the other hundreds of real estate agents he has met. Much to John's surprise, after a few moments of rummaging, Blake pulls out a book.

"Found it!" Blake looks pleased at his accomplishment. He heads toward John with the book in hand.

"Here ya go ... this is for you."

John tilts his head with a furrowed brow, his eyes on the book. He reaches for it.

"What's this?"

"It's a book. You read, don't you?"

Blake is smiling from ear to ear. John smiles as he takes it, realizing it must sound like a silly question. It's not that he doesn't know what a book is, it's that no one has ever randomly handed him one at a car wash. Especially out of the back of their trunk. The book title is *Reinventing Yourself.*

Being an avid reader, he chuckles in recognition of how funny the question must sound. "Yeah, I read."

Blake doesn't miss a beat.

"Well, my dad said 'Give this to some sharp guy, if you ever meet him,' so I'm giving it to you."

Blake's dad is Steve Hardison, a world-renowned personal, business, and relationship coach. Steve Hardison is also Blake's coach.

This is all unbeknownst to John, whose curiosity is piqued as he takes the book into his hand.

Blake says, "Take care, man. It was nice talking to you."

"Thanks for the book. It was nice talking to you too."

There is a distinct and palpable liveliness present between them as they part ways. They both feel something of significance has just happened, but can't put their finger on it. Blake zips out of the carwash driveway excited by the chance meeting completely forgetting his wife Maryn is still there vacuuming out her car. She watches him as he drives away, chuckling to herself knowing its Blake being Blake. She finishes up her business and heads home shortly after he does.

John's car ride to his house is short and reflective. His thoughts are of the chance meeting at the car wash and the current state of life changes he is undergoing. As he pulls into his driveway the book catches his attention. He grabs it and walks inside.

John doesn't just read books. He also uses them in an interesting way. When he wants to hear "what God has to say" about his life at any given time, he'll hold the thought, or feeling, or question in his heart, really feeling it, and then open a book at random and see what that page has to say to him.

Today that book happens to be *Reinventing Yourself,* and the question pertains to the current state of his unexpected, unpleasant reality and the uncomfortable feelings that are going along with it. He flips the book open to a quote from Horace Walpole that says, "Life is a comedy for those who think, and a tragedy for those who feel."

In the quietness of his own home John mutters to himself, "Huh … well I'll be."

The quote strikes a chord, completely flipping him around. In a few simple moments, with a few words of wisdom, he is no longer feeling sorry for himself. Suddenly, as if on cue, poof! Blake's business card falls from the back cover with his contact information on it. John bends down and grabs it. He is compelled to tap out a quick thank you email to Blake from his phone, "Thanks for the book. It's changed the way I'm seeing stuff right now. I really appreciate it."

It's now Monday morning. John is sipping his morning cup of espresso, checking his emails, when up pops a response from Blake. He clicks it open.

"Hey John, the book is from my dad, not from me. Why don't you thank him?" Attached at the bottom is his dad's contact information. John glances at it, not taking it into serious consideration to reach out. Blake's invitation is not a top priority at the moment. He shoots Blake a quick response thanking him again and lets the whole thing go.

It's been a few days since his correspondence with Blake. John is in his car headed up the road to Timney USA, his manufacturing company. He has his phone in hand, stopped at a stoplight, searching for a song he wants to play while he's driving. Ring! Up pops Blake's name on the caller ID. The timing couldn't be more perfect. "Hmmm … might as well." He figures he has nothing to do right now other than to drive. Plus, the conversation at the car wash with Blake was invigorating. He takes the call, "This is John."

Blake's vibrant voice comes through loud and clear on the bluetooth. "Hey, John! Blake here. How are you doing?"

John smiles as he accelerates from the stop light with the purr of the Porsche engine in the background.

"I'm amazing!" Anyone who knows John Vehr knows this is almost always the truth for him. He has unquenchable thirst for the beauty of life and shares it everywhere he goes.

Blake proceeds. "I don't need much of your time. Do you have a moment?"

"Why sure." There is lightheartedness in John's voice. He really likes this kid.

"I was calling to see if you had a chance to call my dad?"

"Nope, I have not."

Blake continues with an encouraging tone. "Give him a call. Thank him. I think you guys will enjoy talking."

With that, things shift gears a bit for John. A couple of days ago the suggestion didn't land. Today it has.

"I'll consider it Blake. Thanks for the call."

Out of pure curiosity, once John arrives at his shop, he pulls up Steve Hardison's website at www.theultimatecoach.com and begins looking at his Curriculum Vitae. He is struck by what it says. Steve, Blake's dad, worked at Rodel Products Corporation for 10 years and held the position of president from 1989-1992. The light in John's head begins to go off. "Well that's fascinating. He must know Don Budinger." Don Budinger, the owner of Rodel Products, was one of John's most influential business and life mentors some years back. Don had impeccable timing showing up in John's life. He came at just the right time, coaching him powerfully in the ways of the world. His impact was life changing, having a profound impact both professionally and personally. He assisted John in shaping him into who he is today. They have not spoken in years, but John has always held him in fondness.

"What are the odds? President of Rodel? Really?" John's curiosity is now beyond piqued. The coincidences keep on rolling in, looking more like synchronicity. He closes Steve's website and goes about his day, busy at the shop but his thoughts are not far from the new events that have transpired. On his way home he decides to give this Steve Hardison a call. Steve is free and able to answer.

"This is Steve."

"Hi Steve. This is John Vehr. I met your son Blake at the car wash last weekend and he gave me a book called *Reinventing Yourself* written by Steve Chandler. I wanted to thank you for it."

"You're welcome. It's a great book written by a great man."

John slows down for a stoplight. "I am reading it now and enjoying it." There's a moment of silence before John continues. "I was looking at your CV today and noticed you were president of Rodel?"

"Yes. That's accurate."

"I assume you know Don Budinger?"

"Yes. For many years now. We worked very closely at Rodel. May I ask how do you know Don?"

"Don was one of my key mentors years ago in both business and personal matters. It was a life changing experience. No matter what he touched—a human being, a home, a business, a foundation—he always made it better for having been part of it, a great guy.

"What a small world. Yes, he is a great guy."

At this point John is impressed with Steve and knows he would like to meet with him in the very near future.

"I'd love to talk to you in person Steve, do you have some time?"

"Yes, I do. Do you live here in Arizona?" The question isn't unreasonable. People travel from all over the world to coach with Hardison. He only coaches face to face.

"Yes, I live locally. In Phoenix to be exact."

"How about meeting next Tuesday at 2:00 p.m?"

"That works great for me."

John pulls up to Steve's house with the rumble of his Porsche Panamera announcing his arrival. It's another bright day in good ol' Arizona. The sun is shining with an inspiring brightness. Steve opens his door, walking out to greet John as he makes his way up the front path. John is a stylish, good-looking man. He is always dressed to the tee even though it rarely leaves the realm of casual. On most days you'll find him with a pair of cargo shorts, t-shirt, and flip-flops. Today he steps it up a notch and wears a pair of Buckle jeans that make his hind end look like something out of a modeling calendar. (Something I will soon be blessed to love and appreciate.)

"I assume you're John." Steve has a bright smile from ear to ear, proving the apple does not fall far from the tree.

"Yes I am."

"Come on in." Steve is gesturing to his open front door. "Feel free to take a seat anywhere you like."

His living room is cascading with sunlight poring in from the large picturesque windows that open to a gorgeous desert terrain. John takes a seat on the couch and Steve sits across in close and comfortable proximity.

"Tell me a little about yourself John."

John and Steve have an immediate rapport, opening a conversation that goes on for close to forty minutes, which is paused temporarily by Steve's wife Amy coming in from her day. Hearing the rustling of bags as she enters through the garage door, Steve rises to go assist his wife. "Will you excuse me for a moment?"

"Of course." John is impressed with his thoughtfulness.

"Hi honey, let me help you." He is taking the bags from Amy's hand. Steve greets his wife with a kiss. "It sure is nice to see you." It's obvious there's endearing love between them, after thirty-five years together that is something special.

"Amy, I would like to introduce you to John Vehr." John rises, joining them in the kitchen with hand extended to shake hers. "Nice to meet you Amy."

"Likewise, John."

Steve offers to take their previous conversation elsewhere for a little privacy. "Hey, why don't we go out to my office." The conversation continues at the same cadence it had before.

After about five or ten minutes, Steve opens it up for authenticity. "John, do you know who you are?"

John tilts his head. "I don't know, tell me."

"Well, I don't want to offend you." Steve's check-in is appreciated but not necessary. John lets him know where he stands.

"There's no way any human being can offend me. Someone could hurt me with a baseball bat, but unless I let them in, there's no way they can hurt me emotionally, right?"

Steve's in alignment with what John just said.

"Yes, as I see it there's no way any other person can offend us, unless we give permission to be offended."

"Yep, so there's no way you can offend me. Go for it." John gives a smile that twinkles a mischievous eye.

Steve pauses, then says, "Alright—you're a smart rat."

John looks playfully perplexed.

"What the hell does that mean?"

Steve continues. "Scientists build these mazes. They'll put an entry and an exit, and they'll put cheese in the middle of the maze. You're the guy who always finds the exit. You're the guy who always finds his freedom."

John lights up, knowing that to be true.

"Yeah, that sounds about right."

Steve drops the bomb: "But you've never found the cheese!"

John's mind has just been blown.

"Wow, Steve … I've never had someone figure me out before."

John is fascinated by how we go through our lives like fish going through water, never seeing what it is we project out into the world. Our perspective is our perspective. And for the most part, we think that's what reality is, but it's not. It's just the water we swim in, and we believe our thoughts about it. When Steve was able to show him the actual reality he had been swimming in, he knew he was meant to work with this man.

Because John has always been a powerful, confident person, not many people have the courage to talk straight to him like this. He really appreciates the authenticity.

"I really want to work with you, Steve."

"Well," Steve says, "I don't have time."

There goes another blow to John's mind. Not only is he used to getting what he wants, but if you saw what Steve charges, you'd say, "That's crazy! No time to accept that kind of money?"

But John persists. He knows that there is a bigger purpose to their working together than John getting what he wants or Steve making money.

"But I really want to work with you."

Steve sees his commitment.

"Okay, I've got an ongoing engagement from 2:00–4:00 on Thursday afternoons that is ending in ten weeks. You're welcome to have that time."

"Excellent!"

CHAPTER 38

A fleeting thought comes to me

The first month of the second year of school is already over and I have nothing set in motion, other than being in overwhelm.

I feel as if I am wallowing around in la-la land with my head stuck in the ground like an ostrich. Ron and Mary have often said that as we make movement on the Goal Line (the horizontal, linear line of worldly achievement), material on the Soul Line (the vertical line, which is the journey of the spirit upward) will come up.

I am up against a serious wall. I've made great progress, and healed on every deep level, but I'm still lacking self-worth. I still believe the voice of my ego saying that I am not brilliant, I am meant to play small and not shine.

Fortunately, God has other plans in store for me and my second-year project will soon begin to serve to pull that forward. USM states that this will be *a project with heartfelt meaning that will make a difference.* That's huge. My heart is called to create a worldwide foundation that will powerfully serve humanity, awakening others to who they truly are! However, there's a little glitch in this ambitious plan: I must first awaken. I am in the process of opening my eyes, but I'm still not there yet.

And, there's another little glitch, I am to come together

with *him,* my life partner, the one I've always known about in my heart.

Call me a hopeless romantic, but for as long as I can recall I've known I was meant to meet someone of significance.

I think we have many soulmates. Some are obvious and some are disguised. Some are even four-legged furry friends! And if you really get down to it we're *all* connected.

But for me, I have also known someone in particular lives in my heart, and that we will come together for a purpose greater than ourselves. However, in my current state of reality, rebounding from the dysfunctional relationships I've had, this coming together is nowhere on my conscious radar. In fact, after my experiences with DJ and Wade I have almost given up on the notion of this soulmate being a reality. Sometimes I even think I'm crazy for believing he exists.

But I am so glad, looking back, that my disbelief did not matter. It didn't have any effect on the synchronicity that kept on rolling me forward. I may be blind to seeing what is now happening, blind to his presence as it ever so steadily approaches my life, but that is okay. It is all with purpose.

So now I am sitting face to face with Joanna Jenkins, my project reader, an angel for sure. Every USM student is assigned a project reader to assist him or her through this process. She is mine.

"Hi Jody, I wanted to see you to talk to you about your second-year project. I know you are feeling overwhelmed and I am here to support you in any way I can."

I am relieved by her kindness. She is absolutely correct about my being overwhelmed.

"Thanks Johanna. I sure am going through it. I am having a really hard time getting clarity of which direction to go."

"Tell me what's going on."

"Well, as you have read in my reports, my heartfelt

intention is to create a worldwide foundation that will assist in the awakening to Love."

Her beautiful blue eyes are set on mine with compassion. After thirty-five years at the University of Santa Monica I'm sure she recognizes my struggle.

I continue. "I just don't see how that is possible, given the time frame. I have no idea where to even begin." I begin to tear up.

"Jody, your intention is beautiful and I encourage you, but Spirit's timing is sometimes different than ours. Given who you are, and what I have experienced of you throughout the last year or so, manifesting a world-wide foundation is a great possibility for you in your lifetime."

She pauses, checking in with me to see if her words are landing. I am all ears.

She says, "What is coming to me is to remind you that life is a *process*, awakening is a *process*. So what would be a stepping stone that would facilitate heading in the direction of creating a foundation? How could you create your project to support you more fully stepping into your authenticity? By doing so, the path to such things as a worldwide foundation will become apparent."

Her questioning pokes my ego and starts bringing up my anxiety. I begin to fidget. I am drawing a blank. I don't have an immediate answer for her. I am up against all my insecurity, feeling like a failure. It feels like my project is not coming to me with grace and ease as it seems to be for so many of my other classmates. I am beginning to wonder what is wrong with me. I think back to the prayerful moment in my bed right before school started. I close my eyes and in the silence of my own mind send a request. "Where are you God? I thought you said it would become clear?"

Days pass, and today I'm back home. I still don't have

clarity on the "stepping stone" Johanna asked about. We agreed to some steps to take this month that will assist me. But I find myself frustrated and irritated. The only thing that keeps me sane is working out. I often ride the stationary bike at the gym and read my books for school as a means to kill two birds with one stone.

Today I have in hand *Time Warrior,* by Steve Chandler. A book that will change my life in more ways than one. I am frantic from a crazy day at work. I have zipped into the locker room, quickly changing my clothes, and now about to head out onto the gym floor to stake my claim on a stationary bike. Before I go, like a gentle breeze, I hear a faint thought coming to me: "Sweet Angel ... your soulmate is near." The faint whisper I hear gently drowns out the sounds of the busy locker room. My breath is taken away. I close my eyes. "Are you willing to open your heart when he arrives?" Whoa. The question catches me off guard. It's a nanosecond of existence bringing me to a full stop.

The reality of what I hear is palpable. I place my hand to my heart, feeling the familiar love and respond. "If what you say is true and that he, the one I've always known, is coming into my life, yes, I am willing to open my heart."

As quickly as the thought came the thought is gone. What just happened is the very definition of a *fleeting thought.* But I haven't lost its importance. In the moment, I was aware ... I answered and I committed.

Once that moment was gone (on the wings of heaven), I did not think about it again.

That is, until he arrives.

CHAPTER 39

Setting an unbelievable intention

I seem to be pedaling the bike faster than normal today without even consciously knowing it. I am so engrossed in this *Time Warrior* book that nothing else seems to exist. It's blowing my mind. *Non-linear time management? How interesting. Slow down to get more done? Cognitive style?*

These are things I have never heard of nor considered as tools for being productive. Up until this point I have been a go-go-go kind of person, believing that being busy is always better. I love what this book proposes! As I read on, something else jumps off the page at me. In passing, there is a mention of the author's life coach, Steve Hardison. There's not a lot of to-do about it, but for me it's as if the words are lighting up on the page. I pause, going back to reread the words: *My coach, Steve Hardison ... at theultimatecoach.com.*

My mind lights up again. *Hmmm, what is that? Why do I feel drawn to that name?* There is a gentle nudge to my heart. It feels like my angels are standing beside me asking me not to dismiss this intuitive hit. Yet, I do dismiss it. My busy mind will not allow for the landing. For now, it's busy attending to all the other fleeting thoughts in the holding tank of my consciousness.

I've always known that my intuition is a blessing, serving as a frequency rod through which I can receive information from the Divine. The only thing is, I have yet to be able to hone it in with any accuracy. Most hits just come and go. It's like an AM/FM radio dial. The channel of connection I am attuned to may be 99.9 but my mind is scanning all over the place receiving information from the whole spectrum.

My thirty minutes are up on the bike. I close the book and jump off, heading straight to the free weights, not giving another thought to this Steve Hardison fella. As I power through my workout, music pumping through my headset, I turn my attention to trying to figure out what my next steps are with my school project.

By now the phrase "life coach" keeps coming to me. Not only by way of its mention in *Time Warrior*, but also from others at school who have shared publicly their choice to make a career change to life coaching as the basis of their project. Feeling a little desperate for a project that fits for me, I reluctantly begin to entertain the thought for myself. I have to decide by the next class, so I am a little at my wits end. Up until now, I have had it in my mind that life coaching was some airy-fairy, hippy-dippy kind of profession. But, as it will turn out, nothing could be further from the truth.

Days continue to roll by and I'm once again on the bike at the gym blowing off steam. I have the same book in hand as I pedal away. This time when I notice the author making another mention of his coach, I cannot ignore my mind and heart lighting up. *There it is again, what's going on?* It's the second subtle mention of his coach, Steve Hardison. Once again the words seem to light up on the page. *What is it about that man's name?* Every time I come across it something inside of me stirs.

I shake my head, redirecting my energy, assuming I am making something out of nothing. But now there is a third mention: *My coach at theultimatecoach.com,* poof! I am locked onto the Light with an undeniable inner recognition. *Okay, that's it! That's the third time. I get the message. I have to at least check out his website.*

Once I am home, I plop down on my bed and grab my funky, half-working laptop. I press the on button and go grab some water. It seems to take an eternity for my computer to boot up so I have time for a little break. I come back to the Google screen up and running. I type in *Steve Hardison - The Ultimate Coach.* Up pops the link and I click on his page. First impression: I am struck by the simplicity, the elegance, and the authenticity. Then these words jump off the page and straight into my heart:

Most coaches have a script or a program. These coaches buff, tweak, and improve your life or your business – a little. I change lives. I have no set curriculum because you are my material. My program is in your speaking.

You speak. I listen. We dance. Your life ignites.

Oh my Gosh! The clarity I've been seeking is right here inside the words he has written. Experiencing Steve Hardison's website has sent me through the roof. I am now thinking I am meant to be a coach. *If this is what coaching is all about I'm all in!* Other latent gifts begin to stir as if they were waiting for just the right moment to make themselves known: *I am meant to work with this man.* My world has suddenly opened to a whole new outlook.

As I absorb the information on his website, I see clearly how coaching and being coached is a powerful stepping-stone to making a meaningful contribution. There are moments when I know, without a doubt, that I know something. This is one of those moments. I click the link to his clients' tributes and get lost in the energy of their positive expression of the profound impact he has had in their lives. One client's posting really captures my attention. He shares the following quotation:

> *"Come to the edge" he said.*
> *They said, "We are afraid."*
> *"Come to the edge," he said.*
> *They came. He pushed them.*
> *And they flew.*

Wow! I love that! The same client also shared words by Rumi that hit home:

Today, like every other day, we wake up empty and frightened. Don't open the door to the study and begin reading. Take down a musical instrument. Let the beauty we love be what we do. There are hundreds of ways to kneel and kiss the ground.

The breeze at dawn has secrets to tell you. Don't go back to sleep. You must ask for what you really want. Don't go back to sleep. People are going back and forth across the doorsill where the two worlds touch. The door is round and open. Don't go back to sleep.

I cannot recall ever feeling the way I do in this moment. SO LIT UP! I eagerly click the link to his contact page, wanting to know how to reach him and how much it is to work with him. *What's the most he can charge?* I am thinking optimistically. I scroll slowly down the page in no way prepared for the answer to that question. My eyes lock onto the page as I read: *Minimum Coaching Agreement: 100 hours (approximately one year), $150,000 - Serious Inquiries Only*

My stomach drops.

"Serious Inquiries Only —$150,000 per year up front? Face to face in Arizona once a week?! WHAT?!" The world has just collapsed around me.

I begin to panic. I am so clear this is meant to be. But how? $150k?!! I don't even know what to do with this information.

I've never even *seen* $150k, nor do I think I ever will in my life. *Really God, I am living at home with Mom, making $15 an hour, just coming through bankruptcy, and this is what shows up as an absolute YES in my world? Tell me how this is going to manifest.*

I hear a faint whisper to trust. But I am irritated, trembling with a slight film of sweat all over my body. It may seem like an overreaction, but in the time I spent visiting his website my dreams had come to life. Now, I am face to face with the inner obstacles that are currently blocking hope. I am ignoring what I have learned at USM these last year or so: with Spirit, all things are possible.

I close my computer, tuck it under my arm, and go downstairs to tell my mom about what has just happened. She is always such a great sounding board. I open the sliding door and join her outside on the porch. She closes her book, sets it on the table, turning to give me her full attention.

I tell her everything. The high hopes, the inner recognition.

"You checked out the coach's website? The one from the book?"

"Yep … and Mom I know I am meant to be a coach and even crazier, I know I am meant to work with him! But the problem is he is super-expensive. Like, way more expensive than I could have ever imagined."

I now have my computer open showing my mom his website. She's into it. Scanning the first page, then clicking on the tributes page. After about ten minutes she nods her head.

"I can see how you would think you're meant to work with him. Totally up your alley. How much is his fee?"

I cringe as I'm answering. "$150,000 … up front."

"Whoa! That's a lot of money, Jod. Unless you win the lottery, not going to happen"

I don't let her words sway me.

"Someday I will work with him. I don't know how or when

I will work with him, but I will."

My clear intention has been set. I close my computer. I can tell my mom is not sold on this ever happening, despite my gung-ho attitude. I can't blame her. Manifesting money (thus far) has not been my forté.

CHAPTER 40

A brave manifesto
is created

Now let's roll back a bit in time. It's June of 2011. It's been a few months since John Vehr first began coaching with Steve Hardison.

And there's good news, even beyond what John expected. His life is taking off in ways he never imagined. His relationship with his kids is growing and expanding. His company is booming to new heights. There is a richness in his everyday relations that is propelling everything forward that wasn't present before.

It's Thursday afternoon.

John is making his now-routine drive to Steve's office. With the top down on his R8 Spider he is rocking out to some hopping music, zipping his way down the freeway grateful for his life: "Man this car is fun! Not bad for a guy who barely graduated high school."

Flashing across his beautiful face is an adorable half-smirk, a smile I will someday be blessed to love. Even on the darkest of days this man could light up anyone simply by being himself. God has blessed him with an energy that glows like walking sunshine.

He has arrived at Steve's and taken a place in his office to wait for him. He's leaves the door open to allow the beautiful day in.

"Hey man!" John rises from the couch to greet Steve.

"Hey John! How's it going?"

They have built a great rapport over the last several months so this time together is something they both cherish. John sits down and begins to share what's on his mind.

"You know, Steve, in life I'm a pretty successful guy. To outside observers, I know I come across as very successful … beautiful women, fast cars, nice properties. Life's good, right?" There is a pause. "But it's not what I want. Don't get me wrong. I appreciate all that I have. It's just something is missing. I know my God to be an abundant God. I know God would not have put people on this planet without having created the perfect system for supplying everything that anybody could ever want. I so know that to be true. The funny thing is, I realize I am not letting the abundance of love flow through my life."

Steve lights up and says, "Excellent realization, John!" He pauses, leaving room for any thoughts John might like to add. There is only a pondering silence. Steve continues, "May I say something to that?"

"Of course. Please do."

"What you have said is powerful. I'd like to slow it down if you're open to it."

By now, John fully trusts Steve's guidance and agrees to slow it down. The next couple of hours are spent with Steve opening John's awareness to a voice inside his head that is limiting his ability to create the love of his life.

John takes a breath and says, "This is wild Steve. Ever since my early twenties I've been very careful with the voice inside my head. I've known how to talk to myself, consciously choosing to navigate away from negative thoughts. But now, after today with you, I am beginning to see there's another voice, one that is deeper down, more powerful, that is not serving me. Quite honestly, I am shocked by this guy inside because it isn't anywhere near who I know myself to be. This part of me seems like some sort of evil twin, saying all sorts of stupid stuff. My mind is blown."

"This is perfect John. This gives us an access point to some powerful work that will change your life. You'll soon see that what we *speak* comes to be in creation."

The next few months are spent exploring the thoughts in John's mind. With yellow pad in hand, he spends ample time pulling out what this pessimistic voice is saying. It has become his morning ritual to take a few moments to consciously listen to the evil twin inside, writing down what he calls "the truths with a small 't' not the Truths with a big 'T.'"

In between sips of espresso the pen flows: "I'm powerless. Why would she want me? Love doesn't last ... " John pauses, frustrated by what he hears, and places the pen to the pad. "Where does all this come from?" He lets out a heavy sigh hearing Steve's reminder to be gentle and forgive.

Finally the day for a breakthrough arrives.

"How are you doing John?" Steve greets him with his normal infectious enthusiasm but John is feeling stressed, he's at his wit's end.

Steve takes a seat in his chair and then notices a red Frisbee in John's hand.

"I'm okay, Steve. I'm feeling like doing something a little different today." John raises the Frisbee. "Feel like throwing this thing around with me?"

Steve is thrilled. "Do I ever, absolutely! There's a great park just down the street."

With that they both get up and head outside. Steve sees the R8 in the driveway. "Lucky. You brought the R8 today, I say you drive." They both smile as they jump in and take off with the top down.

Soon they are playing in the park. Back and forth through the air the red disc glides. There is something meditative about playing Frisbee, at least for John. The car ride over was rather silent with only a little small talk here and there. Steve continues to hold an open space. He knows that when John is ready, he'll talk.

"You know Steve, I cannot believe how I've been talking to myself and not even knowing it. I have gone to great measures to tend the soil of my mind, making sure to nurture it with positivity. I have known for a long time the creative power of the words we speak and it blows my mind what has been running beneath the surface. I have no idea where all the negativity toward love comes from."

He pauses before throwing the red saucer again. "I'd like to be able to clean up my life and have a deeply loving relationship where I can feel loved and trusted—and trust and love someone else."

They walk toward one another, each taking a seat on the grass.

Steve turns with intent eyes, "I appreciate what you are saying John. And, as you are beginning to see you will never get to the place of intimacy you seek by the way you have been speaking of love. The way you are currently holding it is what continues to bring dissatisfying relationships into your life. I can help you, but you will need to be willing to alter how you're going about things."

There is no hesitation in John: "Not only am I willing, I am committed to making a change."

"Excellent! Let's really begin to take a look at what you've been telling yourself and declare new Truths that will serve you in creating the love you seek. Truths with a big 'T.'"

From here the magic begins. John begins consciously creating himself anew by looking openly at his limiting thoughts, forgiving himself and creating the new Truths that will serve him powerfully. It may sound simple but it's far from an easy task.

Statements such as "I am powerless" do not simply flip into "I am powerful" on their own. But it isn't long before the new Truths are coming through John from a place of divine inspiration. As the coaching proceeds with Steve, a document is created by John called the "Manifesto of Abundance of Love in my Life":

> I am an extension of the one true God
>   and I'm powerful beyond measure.
> I have the amazing ability to create uniquely,
> powerfully, and effortlessly.
> I create new worlds as I see the world through
>   new eyes.
> My purpose has always been within me and reveals
>   itself as I grow.
> I am a master builder of pathways and bridges
>   between myself and others and I'm connected to
>   everything.
> God gave me huge talents and as I listen to my own
>   voice
> I create the world I want to live in.
> Love is abundant, perpetual, and leads to ecstasy.
> I am an extraordinary vessel of love.
> I am Pure Love.
> Love has been waiting for me to grow into it
>   and I'm ready for Great Love.
> I was created to give and receive love and love
>   exhilarates me.
> I am open to receive love and love finds me where I am.
> I am that loving that leads to more love.

Feeling through love is how to love.

God places love in my life and I trust His wisdom.

I was created for a Great Love with an extraordinary
woman.

I run toward scary things and I feel myself getting
closer to Great Love; what a ride!

God is Love; I trust His wisdom.

I have high standards and I will have my heart's true
desire.

She has her reasons for loving me; that's enough!

And now this beautifully spoken commitment is out in
the Universe, is it possible that Jody hears the call with her
heart? Could this have caused her mysterious draw to the
name Steve Hardison?

CHAPTER 41

For God's sake, *Just Hit Send!*

To an unprepared heart, receiving can prove to be a challenge.

But I am no longer unprepared. My journey at USM has beautifully tilled the ground for what is to come. The deep healing I have experienced has prepared the sweet space for true love to enter. Without my willingness to go within and learn to love and forgive myself, this door would not have opened. I'd often heard in life that to love another you must first love yourself. It's true, but I didn't really get that until now.

It's important to note what's about to occur is not something that comes out of thin air. Beyond our spiritual connection, both John and I have consciously created one another and the life we are about to share. Through his work with Steve Hardison he has consciously created the ideal woman, me, hence why I have been feeling him. And through my work at USM, using such tools as Ideal Life Scenes and Living Visions, I have created him, placing into the universe for the highest good my heartfelt desire for the soulmate relationship I've always known. Spirit meets us in our point of action. And boy is my world about to be rocked!

My mom and I are zipping down the freeway heading to Los Angeles for Thanksgiving. I am driving her a little crazy with the constant talk of Steve Hardison. She's about to make a strong suggestion that will alter the course of everything.

"You know, Jod, I have an idea that might help you to possibly work with Steve."

I shoot her a perplexed look.

"Really?"

"Yeah, I was thinking you could just contact him and ask him to be your mentor."

Bomb dropped right on the land mine of all my insecurity and low self-esteem.

"Are you crazy, Mom?! I can't do that. He coaches famous people and authors ... people who matter."

She shoots me a glance looking like she's just thrown up. The look has landed and landed powerfully. "You matter too Jod." We fall into silence.

The humming of the car's wheels is not anywhere as loud as the humming of my mind. First off, my mom never, and I mean NEVER encourages me to take a risk. So, her doing so has really struck a chord and gotten my attention. After a few moments of silence I share my thoughts with her.

"You know Mom, coincidentally, at school, we're working on something called Asking for What You Want. It's about having the courage to *ask*, even when we feel fearful or we think it's unreasonable."

She's looking at me with a twinkle in her eyes.

"Sounds like perfect timing then."

Her suggestion has opened a new possibility for me and there is no turning back. By the time we reach my sister's I am on board and committed to sending Steve Hardison an email.

We pull up in my sister's driveway.

"Okay Mom. I'm going to write him an email and ask him to be my mentor."

She smiles a smile of relief.

"I think that's a great idea."

Loving you. Be blessed. Steve Hardison

Ordered at Shutterfly. shutterfly.com

Who is this woman? She has totally blown my mind.

Now, one would think it's a simple task to tap out a quick email and send it along its way. Not for me. Not in this moment. It's Thanksgiving weekend and I am cuddled on the couch, grinding my mind, tapping away on the computer.

I have been working on the email off and on for four days now. It's not that it's a long several-page deal. It's more that I am in agony trying to decide what it is I want to say.

It's about 10:00 p.m. I am done recovering from a stuffed belly due to too much Thanksgiving leftovers. My sister's house is beginning to settle down with the kids being read to in bed. The stillness of the night is fertile ground for my fear to rise. I have opened the computer to stare once again at the one-page typed letter. And once again, as I read my heart begins to race: *You can't do this! Who are you to think you can ask someone like Steve Hardison to be your mentor. You are not worthy enough ... you're crazy ... who in their right mind ... you see who he coaches and what they paid. No way Spirit, I can't do this! I won't do this to myself. That's it. I'm letting this go.*

The line has been drawn. I fully succumb to fear. I slam the computer shut. I'm feeling the tug of God on my heart, but I ignore it. *I will not reconsider. Good Night.* With that I turn off the light, throw my head on the pillow and cuddle up with my resistance and shame. It's comfortable. It's what I know.

When the morning comes, I pop my eyes open, taking in a slight breath of air. The newly rising sun is cascading through the curtain feeling as if it is caressing my soul. I am not fully present yet. I am still in total recall of a dream I just had, remembering I was with angels standing hand in hand in unity. They were encouraging me. There is stillness in the air that fills the room with life. As I lay my head back on the pillow the familiar warmth comes over me. I hear a loving voice, "Sweet Angel ... " There is gentleness to the words that I have never experienced before. I listen openly. "This is much bigger than you are currently aware of. There is a greater purpose to what is going on."

I flash on my refusal to send the email. I begin to tear up, feeling as if the sunlight pouring into the room is healing my fear. The voice continues, "I know you are afraid. You're not alone. Will you reconsider sending the email?"

As I hear the words I become unwavering in my trust: "I hear you God. And, yes ... I'll send it."

It feels as if the room is dancing with Divine entities rejoicing in my commitment of heart and soul. With that I peacefully fall back to sleep.

Now, here's the thing. It's been a day since that beautiful morning and I am now sitting at my desk with the email all ready to go and guess what? (I bet you've guessed it.) I AM *STUCK*. Yep, *toooootally stuck*. The arrow is hovering above the send button and I KNOW there is not one more word I can change. Spirit has clearly given the sign that this is complete. It's a GO. All I've got to do is press the damn button, but here I sit, blankly staring, frozen in space.

To further compound things I am hearing a bunch of naysayers whom I work with filling my head with such negativity, saying things like, "You're crazy, he'll never get back to you. Why would you think about doing such a thing. That's a stupid idea."

I don't know what else to do so, I call my mom. She answers quickly. She knows today is the day I am sending it.

"Hi Mom."

"Hi Jod." I can tell she is waiting for me to tell her I sent it.

"What are you doing?"

She has a playful tone, she knows full well that I am procrastinating.

"Well, you know ... just sitting here ... staring at my

computer screen."

"You haven't sent it yet have you?"

My mom is seriously at her wit's end with this Steve Hardison guy. She knows I am up against my own resistance and low self-worth. She sighs and then something surprising happens. She gets stern and pushy. SO unlike my mom: "JODY ANN SPRECHER *JUST HIT SEND* ON THAT DAMN EMAIL OR I WILL STALK YOU ALL DAY ON YOUR PHONE UNTIL YOU DO."

She has lit the fire under my butt and without further hesitation I hit the button. SWOOSH!

"Oh my gosh! I did it!"

My mom sighs again.

"Thank God. Finally."

Now, what I won't know until later is that my mom is having her own anxiety about all of this. She is afraid he will never get back to me and worried about what that will do to my self-esteem.

"Oh my Gosh Mom, I feel like I have won a huge battle! No matter what, even if he doesn't get back to me I faced a fear. That is huge."

Learning to Fly

CHAPTER 42

It's a great time to learn to fly

The email has landed on Steve's end:

Hello Steve,

My name is Jody Sprecher. I am currently a second year student at the University of Santa Monica. I've been guided to your work by a book I am reading called the Time Warrior by Steve Chandler. When he spoke of you in his book there was an immediate resonance within me to contact you. I am thoroughly inspired after reviewing your website, especially after reading the beautiful tributes others have given. From their heartfelt words it's become clear why Spirit has led me to contacting you. I believe we speak the same language.

I am two months into my second-year project at USM. It's an intense yet beautiful and life changing process. It's gifting me with clarity I've longed for all my life regarding my heartfelt contribution to the world. I've always known I am here to be of service as a pioneer of consciousness. I have held an unwavering dedication in love to bringing that service into form somehow.

Until now, I've only ever known it as a guiding call of my heart with no clear picture of what it would look like. Now, with the tools and experience of USM, I am finally waking up to a newfound clarity and inspiration that the picture is that of being a dynamic life coach.

I've been very resistant to send this email off to you. I feel like I am all over the place. If you're reading this, then it's a fantastic sign of my courage. I've had it typed for days and have hesitated to hit send, stemming from Learning Line opportunities that are arising around my false sense of self-worth, difficulty in asking for what I want, and the lack of financial means to request your services.

Saturday night I had a dream that has inspired me to trust and have faith in moving forward with sending it to you. In the dream, I was holding hands with Angels in a large auditorium where we were elevating the consciousness of humanity by sending out encouragement both telepathically and through vibration of tones via our intention and essence. I woke as the sun was rising, filled with gratitude, energy running through my being as if I had just received a message from Spirit to trust. It is my wholehearted intention to co-create my project (and life) with Spirit. I've always done so every step of the way.

What is clearly coming forward is that a key part of my stepping into the shoes as a coach, mentor and pioneer of consciousness is working with another that will help facilitate the birthing of my gifts and talents. It is also clear that it is not just anybody that I will do this with. There is someone specifically I am meant to work with. I'm not sure if that's why I'm being led to you. It could be you are possibly a touchstone between me and the person I am to work with. All I know at this moment is I feel a strong sense there is a purpose to us connecting and to the fact it's been in my heart to contact you.

Honestly speaking, I feel very vulnerable writing this letter to you and being so open. I feel like I am coming way out of left field. (I know – judgments) I have attempted to write this from a different space. One seeming more "professional" and it doesn't flow. So, I am going with it. I trust this is all part of the process. I feel as if I am standing on a cliff within my consciousness and it's looking pretty freaky but I am jumping anyway. It's a great time to learn to fly. :-)

If any of what I have shared resonates with you and working together in some capacity is a possibility, it would be a great honor to do so. I am open to being creative. As I mentioned earlier there is something in my heart that tells me your journey as a coach, your journey on the road less traveled, the road not for the faint of heart, has gifted you with wisdom to share that would not only be pivotal in regard my path as a life coach, but to other life coaches as well and those we would coach in return. The word that comes to heart to sum it all up is synergy. I've always known this time around, the journey was all about that.

I thank you kindly Steve, with all my heart. I look forward to hearing from you. I send much Light and wish you a happy, belated Thanksgiving.

Kind regards,

Jody Sprecher

CHAPTER 43

A life-changing conversation occurs

As I arrive back from a good long walk at lunch a wave of knowing comes over me. It's a little breathtaking. I stop and turn to my dear friend and co-worker Rachael.

"I think he may have already gotten back to me."

"What? How do you know Jody?"

I close my eyes for a brief moment, "I just got a wave of something that told me so."

By now it's clear as day to Rachael I beat to a different drum.

"It wouldn't surprise me, Jody. This is how things roll for you. It would be a total Jody moment."

She smiles and opens the door offering for me to go in first. What she is referring to by a *Jody moment* is synchronicity. It seems to flow effortlessly and the more I heal and get out of my own way the more I can witness it. I believe we all have access to this way of being, we simply need to tap into the awareness of it.

I race back to my desk with fifteen minutes left on my lunch break. I pop open my email taking notice of the fluttering of my heart. My stomach drops. The top response is from him. "OH MY GOSH! He already responded!!" My heart bursts wide open. I wasn't rejected. I begin pacing around my desk like I am doing some sort of Native American dance. All I need is feathers on my head and it would be complete.

I sit back down. I have my hands to my face taking in deep breaths and letting them out between my fingers. I haven't mustered up the courage to open it yet. I pick up the phone and call Rachael, who is now at her desk downstairs. By now I am making a bit of a commotion.

"Rachael! He responded!"

She gasps, "Oh my gosh! Exciting! What did he say?!"

"I don't know. I'm scared to open it."

"Don't be silly! Open it. I'll be on the phone with you while you do it."

"Okay."

I plop down in my chair moving the cursor over his email. *Click.* Up it pops. I read it aloud to Rachael, my heart thumping in my chest.

> *Jody,*
> *I love who you BE. Thank you for your courage and your generous heart.*
> *I have a client today that is flying in from LA. We will be together from 2 to 4ish MST. Please call me after 4:30 MST today and I will have a few moments and we can talk. (I am the world's slowest typist.)*
> *Please confirm.*
> *Be blessed-Steve*
>
> *p.s. Please watch the long version of this video* *http://www.tbolitnfl.com/p/photos.html*

"Oh my goodness Rachael! He wants to talk!"

The reality of everything begins to sink in. My mind begins to flip and flop with racing fears that truly have no grounding. *I can't talk to him!* At this point I have Steve Hardison on a pedestal. (In the future, I won't. He himself will help me clear that up. I will eventually realize that he is only a mirror reflection of my own brilliance. Whatever we find beautiful, inspiring, and magnificent in another human being is simply our own soul saying hello to itself. But for now, he's on the pedestal.)

Rachael says, "Sure you can talk to him! Don't be silly. This is very exciting Jody."

My heart sounds like Thumper is in my chest. Hardison's acknowledgement has spun me into a 180. No matter what, my life has now changed. Courage has opened a door to a whole new world. By choosing the high road in the face of inner adversity I welcomed miracles of Spirit.

"It's scary Rachael, but yes, very exciting."

Even with the flip and flop of my ego chatter there is a part of me that is calm, knowing, and trusting. I hang up with her and immediately call my mom.

"Hello?" My mom's sweet voice is music on the other end. She hardly finishes before I blurt out what has happened.

"MOM, he responded!" I can feel her relief and surprise.

"WOW, really?! That was fast! What did he say?" Her voice is filled with gentle excitement.

"He offered to talk this evening. And, of course, even though I am scared I cannot pass up the opportunity to do so. This is a big deal, Mom. Doesn't get any more clear of an opportunity to ask for what I want."

"It sure doesn't. Just be yourself, Jod. You are an amazing woman."

It's 5:25 p.m. (4:25 p.m. Arizona time) and I am sitting in my car in a Starbucks parking lot waiting for the clock to hit 5:30. Time is moving slowly. The only thing I know to do is take in deep breaths. I close my eyes for a moment of prayer. "Dear God. I call myself forward into your loving light. May you fill me with peace, love, and confidence. I ask that you bless this conversation with your grace. I pray that all that transpires be for the highest good. I open my heart to you. May Thy will be done. Amen."

I open my eyes flipping the phone over. It's 5:29. "Oh my!" Thump … thump … thump. I think the beating of my heart is shaking the car. The time flips. It's 5:30. I dial Steve's number with a trembling hand. I place the phone to my ear. One ring. Two rings. Three rings.

"This is Steve."

"Hi Steve, this is Jody."

"Hi Jody, I thought it would be you."

There is lightheartedness in his voice bringing a bit of good humor to the conversation.

He says, "What may I do for you, Jody?"

I begin to fumble around with my words, feeling like a scattered train wreck.

"Well, as I mentioned in my email, I am very drawn to your work and believe you are meant to be my coach."

My heart is racing yet there is a part of me that is at peace and comfortable. The candid truth continues to pour out of me.

"I have always known I have gifts that are lying dormant inside. When I saw your website it hit me clearly that I am meant to work with you and that you will help me to birth them."

I pause, feeling a tad stupid knowing I am about to drop the whole *I have no money so will you mentor me* bomb. Or at least it feels like a bomb in my own mind. I begin to slouch over in my car wanting to crawl of out my skin rather than say the next sentence. I proceed anyway:

"But Steve, I barely have any money and well … " My internal dialogue begins a conflicting clash with my outward words. *Oh my gosh, I can't do this, what am I doing?* The gentle knowing takes over. *Just say it.* "Well, I didn't know if you have any sort of mentoring or internship program. If you do I would love to be considered to be a part of it if possible."

There! I did it. Thank goodness that's over. I wait for his response, pulse rate up and present.

"Jody, as much as I would love to say yes, which I would have done given who you are, but I do not do mentoring."

His voice is kind, clear, and present: "I have a client that has coached with me for over seven years. He is an extraordinary individual and a good fit for you from what you have shared in your email. I'll give you his name and if you're interested, you can contact him and let him know I referred you."

My heart is a little deflated by what he is saying but the knowing is unwavering. There is something profound going on that is beyond conscious thought. I jot down the man's name.

"Thank you for that, Steve."

My mind is spinning. As the moments pass, the conversation effortlessly seems to deepen, my heart opening wider. I can be nothing other than 100% authentic with this man. There is a long pause as I try to find my words.

He says, "What may I do for you? What would you like to create?"

His question has caught me off guard. I have never had anyone ask me that before.

"Well ... do you mean *anything*?"

"Yes, anything. What we speak creates. I am here to be of service to you."

"Well, I would love to create abundance in my life."

As the words leave my lips I am rather startled by them. It feels as if hidden truths are beginning to surface. Steve begins to tell an incredible story of how many years ago a written manuscript with no title mysteriously came into his life. I am glued to his words as I sit in a parking lot in my car with the motor idling, keeping warm from the air blowing from the vents. He continues with his story.

"For many years I did not know who wrote it. I wanted to find out who it was so I could be clean with the fact I had copied it and given it to so many people. Throughout the years I have shared this manuscript with many of my clients. Not only did I want to reimburse the author, I also wanted to thank him or her for their extraordinary work. It wasn't until ten years later that I found out who wrote it. I had a new client come in who lit up when I showed the manuscript to her, saying she had read the book! She shared it is called *How to Solve Your Money Problems Forever* by Victor Boc. I was thankful, for I could finally get in touch with the author and share my gratitude for his work and to make good on the reproduction I had done. It's a book that will change your life. You can get it on Amazon. I encourage you to do so. If you follow what is outlined in it abundance will flow into your life. "

Steve's suggestion sparks my imagination.

"Okay great! Thanks Steve. I am adding it to my second-year project. Thank you for sharing that story with me. It's inspiring!"

The cadence of the conversation continues to flow deeper.

"What else, Jody … How may I assist you?"

The thumping of my heart has calmed a bit as authenticity continues to pour forth with little or no effort.

"Well, if we're creating anything I would like to step into my personal power."

Steve eloquently launches into another beautiful story about his dynamic coaching experience with Deuce Lutui. He shares about how TBOLITNFL came into existence and the profound impact it has had on so many. He is explaining the power of personal internal commitment and what that could mean for me in my life. "I sent you the link to a two-hour video. Watch it as it pertains to you and your personal power will open."

I agree to do so, and commit to including it in my project as well. There is a moment of silence with a peculiar heightening of my senses.

"How else may I serve you Jody?"

His words, though simple, are serving to stretch my boundaries. My original intention for calling him is complete and was completed in the first two minutes of the conversation. Now we're in uncharted territory talking about subjects I had no idea were going to come up. There is a dance with Spirit going on, opening my heart for what is next. Steve helps me along my way:

"Jody, I want to be of service to you. Whatever had you call, or write the email, if you can just tell me what that *really* is. Let's get to that. I want that for you too."

I suddenly look up and see the address of the building I am parked in front of. It reads 111. Always a sign of my angels. His statement bursts my heart wide open. I have never had someone hear me the way he is hearing me or meet me exactly where I am at. There is something in his presence, even felt over the phone, that ignites my mind. There is no more holding back. Surprisingly, the real reason why I wrote the email and called comes flying to the surface. It has made its way through the resistance of my past, and is now coming forth from a sacred place:

"Well Steve, if we're talking about creating *anything* . . . I've always known someone in my heart. My friends and family think I am a hopeless romantic but I can't explain it. Even though we have never met physically I know him. His energy is clear as day to me. It's a profound love for another that has no words." I begin to tear up. "People think I am crazy but I know I am not. I can't explain it other than I know him, I love him, and I will wait. Even if it's lifetimes."

I pause, wiping a tear from my cheek. Then I continue.

"I can't even believe I am telling you this. And, to tell you the truth I'm not even sure if he's here on this earth anymore. I thought by now we would have met but I am beginning to think he may have possibly already made his transition. But I don't know. All I know is the love I know for this person is one you cannot fake or pretend or project onto another. It's unique between us. A gift given from the Divine. A blessing. I know, with all that I am, we have a sacred contract to walk this path together in loving service. Our love is expansive, joyful, and heart-centered."

I am shocked at what's coming out of me. Never in my life have I spoken so directly to another person about the one I love. I have shared bits and pieces briefly, but most of the time, when I do that, people think I have watched too many romance movies.

"And, Steve, if you knew my past with men you wouldn't believe I even hold onto this beautiful possibility. I've been through some serious stuff that would usually break one's spirit toward love. And yet, I stand strong in who we are and I wait patiently."

"Jody, what I'm listening to is the most beautiful space of love and honor for another human being that I have ever heard created. I have never heard another speak as powerfully and beautifully of love as you just did. If you are willing, please capture the essence of what you speak. Write it down as if that person were in the room. What would it look like? Write what you are looking for in a relationship and send it to me."

Lights spark in my mind. *If he were in the room? What I am looking for in a relationship?! I know exactly what I am looking for.*

Bells of recognition go off in my mind like those in a high chapel. *PROMISES.* The angels whisper … *Promises, Promises, Promises.* Each time I hear the word a light bursts forth from a place I have yet to consciously experience until now. Inspiration is surging through my core and I know that I KNOW.

"Steve I know exactly what I am looking for. I will send you something by Sunday."

"Excellent!"

There is another brief pause with yet another profound shift in energy.

"Is there anything else you wish to say, Jody?"

At this point my being is full. Any more and I may burst. I give off a slight giggle, "No Steve, I think I had better stop here."

"Okay great. Then we are complete for now. But before we go is it okay if I say something to you?"

"Yes, please do."

What he says next rocks my world. His voice is crystal clear and seems to be coming from some place greater than himself.

"I'll be at your wedding."

I hear his words and know without a doubt that what he says is the absolute truth. It blows my mind!

"You know, Steve, somehow I know that to be true."

CHAPTER 44

A heart promising to love and be loved

I hang up the phone feeling a little in shock. What just happened?

My hands rest gently on the gearshift, ready to place it in reverse to move from the parking spot I have been idling in for the last thirty minutes. I am taken by the power of the moment. *Could it be? The one I've always known?*

But then I begin to come back down to earth. *Wedding? Wait ... what? I'm not getting married.*

Like a dark nightmare my past with DJ and Wade comes flying into my mind. *Me, married? No way. The patterns of the past do not change.*

But my dreams that night are wild and thrilling, full of brilliant light and waves of love. I know my angels have visited me.

Then, in the gentleness of the next morning, I lie in bed, half-asleep with my dreamer's heart wide open. I pop my eyes open with inspiration surging through me. I sit up, wrapping the covers around me, sensing a light connected to the chord of my being. I know a clearing has occurred in the sleep state. I begin to fumble around for my journal and a candle.

It is just barely sunrise, a rare time for me to be awake in the first place, but I am. And I know that I must put to paper what is coming to me. I find the white candle, flick the match to light it, and place it next to my bed. I grab my journal and my purple pen. What begins to pour forth is a blessing, a calling to the one … the one I would soon know as John. The rain has not stopped for the past two days even for a moment. It's beautiful in how it's assisting me in letting the thoughts and words flow.

Sentence by sentence my heart pours out. I have never experienced anything like this birthing process of my heart's code. Minutes turn into hours of timeless creation. As the final words come through my hand I know I have arrived at completion: *I am promising to love you and be loved by you.*

There! Wowee … complete! Without thinking any further, I tap out a quick email to Steve Hardison:

Happy Sunday Steve,
Okay, so here it is. What I am looking for in a partner. Once again I find myself unable to be anything less than 100% authentic with you. Thanks for bringing my authenticity forward. I am growing fond of these Courageous Cliff jumps. :-)

The only way to share what I am looking for in a partnership is to express from my heart the promise I feel was shared between my soul and another. It's a promise of Love. The melody has played in my heart all my life. In my best attempt to share the energy it resonates, it goes something a little like this …

A Promise of the Heart

I am promising to love you with all that I am and to receiving being loved by you

I am promising to grow together in love learning with an open heart and expanding in joy

I am promising to be your best friend supporting you in becoming the best you can be

I am promising to stand as a reflection of your brilliance and uniqueness inspiring you with love to follow and manifest your gifts and dreams

I am promising to serve as a reminder of your authentically beautiful goodness encouraging you in always shining bright

I am promising to love you unconditionally accepting and appreciating who you truly are in the wonderful fullness of your humanness

I am promising my unwavering love and commitment to the full divine expression of us as a couple and to the full divine expression of us as individuals

I am promising to support wholeheartedly our intimate discovery of each other as Blessings of Love

I am promising you my loyalty always and forever

I am promising my loving commitment to growing together on the Learning Line of life willing to embrace opportunities for growth with love and light

I am promising to create a co-committed relationship where discovering ourselves together is more deeply intimate and authentic than if we are apart

I am promising to bring forward the best in one another growing together in love and friendship

I am promising to walk together in joy through this magnificent journey of life offering an authentic example what it means to BE love and to be in love.

I am promising my whole Self to you in perfect vulnerability so we may share the beautiful blessings our connection is offering

I am promising to share laughter, joy, and heart-centered connectedness

I am promising to listen wholeheartedly and to authentically share my truth

I am promising to always hold and cherish the Holy Spirit as the center of our union

I am promising an openness to the wonderful new depths of intimacy our relationship will bring forward

I am promising to honor and celebrate our humanness in all the many brilliant shades and colors

I am promising to love you and be loved by you

I know my partner as my best friend, lover and companion. We are stronger together as a couple than we are apart growing in ways we never imagined or thought possible. We are each other's rock, each other's best friend and each other's blessing by being one another's catalyst for the next level of our evolution. We are deeply connected through the Love of Spirit.

On a more earthly level I love a great conversation, appreciate having fun and value being physically fit. Ideally he would too. I love nature. I love being outdoors camping, hiking, backpacking, etc. Earth and all her beauty takes me to a deeper level of Home. Ideally he loves nature too. I love to be affectionate. Not overly so with obnoxious displays of public affection but I value closeness and intimacy. Ideally he would too. And obviously being spiritual is a key.

This is a little of what my heart sings to me when I think about my Path Partner. It would be a true Blessing if you hear an echo to it in someone you know. I would probably find myself speechless. :-)

Okay, well wow ... this is two novels I've sent you in a week. :-) I am filled with so much gratitude for you and for you taking the time to listen. That in itself has been tremendously healing and life changing. Thank you so very much. You have a beautiful impact Steve. It's inspiring. I am sending you many blessings of light and love.
Jody

CHAPTER 45

John finds out about Jody

John meets Jody on December 4th.
Jody meets John on December 5th.
How exactly does this happen?

L et's start here: It's the evening of December 4th and Steve Hardison is sitting in his office checking emails. As he scans his inbox he sees my email with the subject titled "Promises." He hovers the mouse cursor and clicks it open. As he begins to read, he is inspired by what I have written.

As he reads on, he suddenly remembers his last session with John. It was the session in which he saw that John has finally had a complete transformation in his ability to be in relationship with a woman. Through his work with Steve, his pessimism has disappeared. His beliefs about the possibilities of love being limited have let go of him. They have been dissolved.

Steve knows that up until now, John was in no way ready to meet a woman like me. Steve thinks further back to a few months prior when he and John were in the painful throes of the creation process of John's Manifesto. John's intention of creating the ideal relationship was at odds with the patterns of his past. Steve recalls that John's old beliefs were dying hard.

Steve remembers one conversation in particular. He had come to his office to find John slouched on the couch with a look of despair.

John said, "Dude you're taking all my toys away! What's going to happen with my life? This is really hard, man."

Steve said, "For the relationship you desire, we're going to have to continue to do a couple of things." He paused. "You have to unplug all the things that are competing with your desire for a loving relationship. How you hold things is still conflicting with your Manifesto. You don't go pick a woman off a showroom floor; you get related to her in a different way."

Steve quickly comes back from memory lane bringing with him the awareness that John gets it. All the great measures they have done to consciously create love anew have paid off. John is now relating to life from the space of his Manifesto.

Steve decides to send John an invitation. He types it and then hits send, *SWOOSH!!* The miracle is now in motion, riding through cyber space, landing only seconds later in John's inbox. John is in his office checking emails before tucking his kids into bed. He immediately sees Steve's email come in. He thinks, "Excellent! An email from Steve is always a treat."

 He clicks it open, in no way anticipating what this one email would do for his life and his future:

John, I received this from a woman I've neither seen nor met. If it interests you, bring it with you on Thursday. We'll discuss it.
Be Blessed, Steve

John then begins to read Jody's Promises. *Happy Sunday Steve, Okay, so here it is. What I am looking for in a partner … .* Her words hit home. They awaken something in him. Halfway through the Promises he begins to feel something very unique … he begins to feel that he is already in love. He reads on:

I am promising my whole Self to you in perfect vulnerability so we may share the beautiful blessings our connection is offering

I am promising to share laughter, joy, and heart-centered connectedness

I am promising to listen wholeheartedly and to authentically share my truth

As he reads, he begins to feel a moderate level of shock. His heart is beating fast, sweaty palms and shortened breath. It's almost like tachycardia.

I am promising to always hold and cherish the Holy Spirit as the center of our union

I am promising an openness to the wonderful new depths of intimacy our relationship will bring forward

I am promising to honor and celebrate our humanness in all the many brilliant shades and colors

I am promising to love you and be loved by you

"Whoa …" His eyes are glued to the computer screen. "I didn't think there was a woman who existed on this planet who knew her heart this well and could be so vulnerable with it."

John's perception of women in the past was not that they were shallow or cruel, but only that they had built tall walls and strong gates around their hearts. With the opening of his own heart during his work with Steve, he realized *we all do this.* So could he ever find a woman without those walls?

John is finally able to take a small breath "She's here …" He sends a quick email response to Steve:

Zowie!

I have to tell you, halfway through reading her words I was having a hard time breathing and my heart was beating fast; I thought it might beat straight out of my chest. I was speechless when I read the word "speechless" because there was absolutely no way I could make words come from my

mouth at that moment. Her honesty, her authenticity is
palpable. I would very much like to meet her.
Loving you,
JDV

John knows nothing (on the worldly level) of the woman whose heart he has just encountered. He has no idea what she looks like, where she lives, or what she does for a living. Nor does he care! All he knows is he has met his soulmate and he has fallen in love.

CHAPTER 46

Jody finds out about John

It's December 5th at 8:00 a.m.

I've arrived at work early, bouncing around the office extending warm greetings to the few co-workers who have also arrived early. I pop my head into the sales office. "Want some coffee, guys?" I hear a muddled and tired response of "Yes, please." I walk to the coffee machine, eager to smell the aroma of roasted beans wafting through the air. I go about my business, completely clueless about last night's email exchanges between John and Steve.

In my current state of mind, I only believe that maybe someday, in years to come, something might happen with the Promises of my Heart. Sending them to Steve Hardison was like writing them in a journal. It was clarifying to do it, but I never expected anything to really come of it.

But Steve Hardison operates differently than other people do. It turns out that he is never one to "sit on" something. A higher vibration guides him, one he trusts wholeheartedly. Little do I know, as I frolic around my office in an oddly good mood, he is about to introduce me to my soulmate.

I take a seat in front of my computer with mellow music playing in the background. Listening to soft inspiring music is one of the ways I stay calm and centered in a less-than-ideal work environment. I sip my morning coffee, pop open my email, and begin to scan my inbox. My eyes are half way down the page when they suddenly come to a screeching halt.

There is an email from Steve Hardison.

"What? I wasn't expecting to hear from him again." My stomach drops. I am not even sure why. "This is a tad surprising, I didn't think we'd be talking again until after my agreements were complete. Hmmm ... " I nervously open it, my mind attempting to rationalize. "I bet he's just saying thank you for my Promises email."

As I go to click the email open, it feels like time has slowed way down.

> *Jody, This is the response I received this evening from one of my clients after sending him your document. What phone number do you want me to give to John?*
> *Be Blessed.*
> *Steve*

In mid sip I about spit my coffee all over the computer screen. *What?! Holy crap!* This was not what I was anticipating. Fear comes rushing in. *How could he send my heart to someone?!* My stomach gives way to the anger as it begins to rise. What is happening has nothing to do with the present. The present is a gift. It has everything to do with the blind haunting of my past. *WHAT?! He shared my heart with someone?! Oh my, NO!*

I place my coffee down on the desk quickly bringing my elbows to rest next to it. I land my face in my hands in an attempt to calm down. My first year at USM is echoing in the background, reminding me I have the skills to work with any negative emotion or judgment. Yet, I am blown away and unable to move. Not only am I now terrified that Steve Hardison comes from the same lack of honor that DJ did, but I am also face to face with my fears of ever allowing love into my life.

I take a breath. Maybe I can slow this down for a moment and shed some light onto these wildly upsetting thoughts.

Maybe this moment is actually a blessing. Maybe my past is

a blessing for having brought me here. Maybe Spirit has heard my prayers and knows I am ready to heal. I'm feeling better now, but my mind continues to race with thoughts of DJ and Wade. Like flashes on a movie reel, I recall the heartache. With each bad memory my heart begins to beat faster and faster.

As I sit here with my face in my hands all of a sudden I hear a familiar soft, reassuring voice: "Sweet Angel … " The gentle kindness comes again to slow the churning of my mind. At first the words seem distant and hard to hear: "Give this a chance Sweet Angel, it is not want you think. You are safe, loved, and guided. Are you willing to see through the eyes of your heart?"

I pull my face from my hands knowing the encouragement I hear comes from a place of sacredness. I am reminded of the beauty of the weekend. "Yes, I am willing." With that my heart opens. Now I'm finally ready to read John's beautiful email and something shifts and awakens.

> *Zowie! I have to tell you, halfway through reading her words I was having a hard time breathing and my heart was beating fast; I thought it might beat straight out of my chest. I was speechless when I read the word "speechless" because there was absolutely no way I could make words come from my mouth at that moment. Her honesty, her authenticity is palpable. I would very much like to meet her. Loving you, JDV*

There is something about John's email that touches me to the core. But the good feeling doesn't last. My unresolved past triggers me. Now I'm focused on a scary possibility: the threat of another Wade approaching. My unresolved past is now casting a blinding shadow on a potential future.

No way, God. I will never let anyone in again … and, how could this Steve Hardison person think it's okay to share my heart with someone?

I am now completely pissed off. I rush down the hallway, hanging my head low, avoiding eye contact with the passing few co-workers along the way. I am headed straight to the bathroom to hide the almost-tears that now are misting around my eyes.

Before I can get to the bathroom door I am stopped by a compassionate coworker.

"Are you okay?"

She sees how upset I am and reaches for my arm. I turn to her gently.

"Yeah, I'm fine."

I look up, giving her a fake half-smile. She can tell it's best to give me space. I rush into the bathroom and close the door behind me. I look into the mirror, "Get it together, Jody."

I talk to myself in an attempt to redirect the feelings. As I stand in the bathroom I begin to see clearly the path of preparation my work has provided. I see how I myself have actually been creating this moment. *Could it be?* My ideal scenes pop into my mind as if they are lighting up on a movie screen. I flash from scene to scene. I recall the living visions I have spoken into creation. One by one I am reminded. I remember the night at the gym when I heard my soulmate was near. I recall being asked if I was willing to open my heart. I was! As the memories pour down like sweet rain the fear begins to subside

I think of Steve Hardison, realizing I over-reacted. If I really think about it, what did I expect? There has been no wrongdoing or violation of trust here. That is all my projection. Here in the simplicity of the moment, as I reframe the events of the morning, I realize the only thing to fear is fear itself.

If I were on my deathbed I would regret not giving love a chance.

I have finally calmed down enough to head back to my

desk. I grab for the bathroom door whispering a quick prayer of gratitude, "Sometimes I think I am crazy for believing in you ... you who I cannot see. But I thank you for all your love and support. I cannot deny the grace that is present. I love you."

With that I open the door, thinking I may be talking to the air (but sometimes the air sure does have a magical way about it!). I walk out slowly and look around like I am in some James Bond movie in full-on stealth mode not wanting to be noticed. Luckily, the coast is clear. I head back to my desk, sit down, and move the cursor on my mouse to get my computer screen to come out of screensaver mode.

John's email is front and center. I reread it. My heart is once again touched. His words are kind and gentle.

I begin to coach myself. "It's just a phone call, Jody. What do I think? He's going to crawl through the phone and kill me?" I chuckle at my own thought. "Wow, emotional triggers can sure knock one off their center." With that, I commit internally to sending an email off to Steve at lunch.

Now it's lunch time and I've canceled my normal walk to send the email off. The words seem to flow effortlessly.

Hi Steve,

Thank you for the introduction to your client. I really don't know what to say. Just as I thought I would be, speechless. After getting over my initial shock this morning of my heart being directly shared with your client (that was better for waking me up than a cup of coffee geeez wow) I was filled with gratitude and a sense of surrendering to the process and saying Yes! to the Universe. John's words are kind and touching. It will be wonderful to connect with him by phone. Here's my number. With a heartfelt gratitude I wish you a blessed day.

Jody - the Courage Cliff Jumper :-)

Without a moment's hesitation I press the send button.

CHAPTER 47

"Why hello,
there you are ..."

Even though I am trying to act like it's no big deal, I notice
I am driving close to eighty mph down the freeway in an
attempt to get home a little faster. I am rocking out to music
and singing at the top of my lungs.

Both acts are strange for me.

When I drive I usually cruise at a grandma speed of about
sixty-five, and I most certainly do not sing out loud.

I pull off the freeway with the pause between songs
allowing room for my thoughts to pop off like popcorn. *It's just
a phone call ... this really is no big deal ... I'm just having a casual
conversation with someone I don't know.* I remind myself not to
get ahead of where I am. *Even if we have a nice conversation he
could be a troll or a freak of some sort.*

Even as the words leave my mind my heart knows none
of what I think is true. There is a greater part attuned to
significance of what is. The curious part of it all is that *there is
NO fear.* I am not comparing to the past or creating a negative
future fantasy. I am centered in the present, feeling alive in
the NOW. What's clear is I have never felt this before.

I pull into my driveway, jumping out of my car with a
little pep in my step. I fly through the front door looking to
my mom like I'm Batman, now setting my stuff down in the
entryway with a bit of a playful thrust. Okay, maybe that's a

little bit of an exaggeration, but the Batman thing sure sounds fun. I'm smiling from ear to ear.

My mom takes notice of my enthusiasm, "I guess he called you?"

"Yep, he did! But I wasn't able to answer. I'm planning to call him back in a few minutes."

She smiles. I assume she's happy to see my glow. I am about to head upstairs, but before I do I stop by the refrigerator to grab some water. I float on by my mom, aiming straight for the stairs. About half way up I hear her calling to me in the background, "Just be you Jody, you're a beautiful woman … and let me know how it goes."

I pop my head under the railing. "Roger that, Mom." I smile from a place I thought I had long forgotten. Once in my room I take in a few long deep breaths, exhaling the residual craziness of the day.

Now I begin to get a little nervous. It's time to return John's call. *What if I have to leave a voice mail? I hate that.*

I sit for a few moments, waiting until I feel completely calm. I am hoping to magically feel like a Zen master might feel. Not quite happening though. I look for my purse, which has my cell phone in it. "Oh dang … " I realize that in my hurrying Batman mode, I'd left my purse by the front door. I quickly hustle downstairs to grab it, flying back up the stairs without a moment's hesitation to once again close the door behind me. I take a quick breath in, click on John's number in the missed call screen, and without any more hesitation I hit send. Away it goes! The call is out.

I place the phone to my ear. One ring. *Oh my.* My heart starts to beat a little more rapidly. Two rings. *Oh double wow.* Now my heart is thumping in my throat. Three rings. *Holy crap!* Now the all too familiar drumming nervousness is going off in every cell of my body. His voicemail picks up.

I say "Oh shit!" But I have to do it. What else am I going to do? Hang up? I must do the dreaded "leave a voicemail" thing.

His greeting is short: "This is John. You know what to do." BEEP.

Oh crap! Here I go. I begin to speak, having no idea what I am saying. My words feel swayed by the beating in my chest. Out flows a jumbled mess of sentences that seem to stumble over each other. (Oh the joys of love.) I say what comes to me as quickly as I can and hang up the phone. I am so nervous I don't even know if I said goodbye. I stand staring down at my phone as if it is a partner in some crime. *What a flustered mess that was.*

I put my cell phone down on my dresser giggling to myself. *Wow, really Jody? It's just a phone call? What happened to your Zen state of calm?*

It's a true sign of my spiritual growth (thank you, USM) that I can laugh at my humanness. It can be quite comical at times.

I go about my business for the next twenty minutes, acting like putting away my laundry is the most important thing I have to do in the universe. I've even put on some great music to try to distract me. But the truth is, my mind and heart are with John.

Suddenly, from the corner of my eye, I see the phone lighting up. There's an incoming call! I grab it, trying to act casual. I see it's his number. I put my hand to my mouth to calm my excitement. Everything is once again going into slooooow motion. I press the receive button and say "Hello?"

There is a pause that feels like the sweet kiss of a long lost lover.

John's voice says, "Why hello, there you are ..."

As much of a cliché as it may be, he has me at hello.

Now, first conversations are commonly of the earthly variety, meaning they are filled with questions such as "What

do you do?" "Where do you live?" and "What do you look like?"
Not ours.

Not that earthly conversation is bad or wrong in any way. I
have them all the time and feel deep gratitude for those I connect
with in light-hearted, trivial communication. It's wonderful.

Our conversation is different. There is a distinct energy
to it that has a life beyond words.

As I've mentioned before, I believe soulmates come in
many different forms. Some show up as family, some as
friends, some as lovers, others as temporary partners to help
us heal. I now know that some even show up as what we
would term enemies. We are all here to serve one another.
We all have that purpose. Sometimes it takes years to realize
the truth of this.

But in the case of John, I know it right now. Right here
in this conversation I have the keen awareness I have always
known him. We had to be ready for this extraordinary
experience we are now in, and that took healing for us both.

Three hours and forty-five minutes later (and, mind you
John HATES the phone), we begin to bring our conversation
to an end. Not because we want to, but because it's getting
late and we know we should. Somehow we slow the magical
energy down bringing it to a conclusion.

"Well gosh, John, I am so thankful we have met. This has
been extraordinary."

"Me too, Jody. I am happy to have met you too. I look
forward to when we speak again."

As we hang up I realize my heart has burst wide open. As I
stand in my room I literally vibrate, feeling open and receptive,
knowing my life has been forever changed. I'm blessed beyond
my dreams.

I sit down on my bed and lower my head in gratitude. "All
I can say is, thank you."

CHAPTER 48

Even my mother can see it now

Over the last few weeks John and I have spent ample time in conversation. Some of our talks have lasted up to seven hours. The other night we had a seven-hour phone date where, much to our surprise, 2:00 a.m. showed up rather quickly.

I am discovering the timelessness between us is here to stay.

I arrive home from another busy day at work. The zoom, zoom, zoom of the workday has me completely foggy headed. As I groggily walk through the front door my mom greets me with a peculiar smile.

"Something came for you today."

She gestures to a package sitting in the entryway. I perk up with interest.

She continues, "I think it's from John. It has a Timney label on it. Didn't you say that is the name of his company?"

By now, I have told my mom about John and who he is to me, although I have not actually come out and said to her that I know in my heart I am going to marry him. I still have kept that at bay, not wanting to worry her, figuring it would come out when it was time.

She does, however, know we share a unique love for one another that is different from any other experience I have ever had. She seems to be genuinely excited for me (which is a first in my love history given the dynamics of my past.)

I turn my head slightly with confusion, "Really, a package from John for me? I don't know about that, Mom. I can't imagine what he could have possibly sent me."

My mom's humor comes out in complete logic. "Well, there is only one way to find out who it's from and what it is, silly."

I giggle, snapping myself out of my serious inquisitive state.

"Right ... that's true ... I guess I'll open it."

I reach for the box feeling like a kid at Christmas. It's fairly large and awkward to handle. I take a seat on the floor next to the Christmas tree, placing it by my side. My car keys are still in hand. I use them to cut along the taped edge of the box. As the keys slice it open I become very curious. The chaos of the day begins to fade away. Finally the side pops open and out flows an amazing white down comforter along with a card with my name handwritten on it. I light up, hugging it close to my chest.

"Oh my gosh! How thoughtful!"

My mom is on the edge of the couch fully present with the moment. "So, I guess you know who it's from?"

I turn to see her smiling. She's making reference to the fact that I haven't opened the card yet. She waits patiently while I snuggle my face for a bit longer into my new delight. Her patience runs out. "Well, read the card, silly." I look over and notice she is totally into this.

I redirect my attention to the little white envelope, noticing that his handwriting is lovely. I peel back the seal, remove the card, and read it aloud. *Jody, This will keep you warm and cozy while I am not there. Love John*

I about burst into tears. "Oh my gosh ... he's so amazing!" I pick up the comforter again, hugging it with all my might. My mom is slightly perplexed over the significance of a comforter but that is outweighed by the pleasure she sees in me. I catch on and fill her in.

"He's so thoughtful, Mom. We were talking one night where I made a brief comment of how I love down comforters but have never officially owned one of my own. And now he sent this as a gift without even telling me. Pretty amazing."

My mom places her hand to her heart. She is touched, "Yes it is very thoughtful, Jody. From what you have told me of him and from his actions he is obviously a kind man … and obviously very much in love with you."

She grabs my hand. "Jod … " She pauses.

"Yes, Mom?"

She looks straight into my eyes.

"You know, Jody, I really think he's the one. The one you've always said you'd meet. I always thought you were a little goofy about believing in such a thing but I don't know. This is different."

"Mom, I have actually known since I heard him say hello. May sound cheesy but true. In that moment I knew I was going to marry him. I didn't tell you since I didn't want you to worry. I know my past has been hard for you to watch me go through. Out of curiosity, what made you say this?"

The look in her eye is one of upmost certainty. "I don't know, I can just feel it in my heart Jod, and know it to be true."

CHAPTER 49

Opening the windows of the soul

"So, when can I come and take you to dinner?"

John and I are having another one of our lovely phone conversations. I am wrapped up in my cozy new comforter lying on my bed with the phone to my ear. There is a flicker of candle flames dancing on the walls as I listen to his voice. Candlelight in the evenings has become a common ritual.

His question triggers my girlie side, sending my thoughts to wanting to be as sexy as I can be. In the silence my mind stirs: *Oh my goodness, come and take me to dinner? I need to get my hair done, my nails done and maybe lose five pounds before we meet.* Of course none of these thoughts are true, but I still let them influence my response: "How about in a couple of weeks ... let's say ... on January 8th?"

There is a moment of silence on his end. Then, "That works. My calendar is open that day."

Even though I am dying to meet him face-to-face I feel a bit of relief as I now have some time to get beautified. But then he shocks me by saying, "And, Jods ... "

"Yeah, John?"

"How about I come and take you to coffee next Wednesday the 28th?"

Oh my gosh! My stomach drops. Was I ready to actually see him in person? My stomach feels as if it's lying on the floor with butterflies fluttering about. Holy crap! He is good! I can hear his endearing *John-ness* coming through loud and clear from the other end. He has this amazing way about him that brings instant access to joy. He is loving, kindhearted, playful, and sometimes mischievous in nature, making him uniquely and beautifully who he is. I find him simply irresistible. My mind flashes to the logistics of his last comment. It's now Friday! That's literally a few days away. I suddenly start giggling, realizing who cares if my nails and hair are not perfect. He doesn't love me because of that. He loves me for who I am. We both know our love for one another, and have spoken of our commitment to a life together. I surrender with excitement. "That sounds great!"

The airplane is cruising through the air, headed due west chasing the good ol' golden rays of the California sunset. John, who is sitting in first class, notices there is only one other couple siting in the cabin with him. They are an older couple sitting to his right, holding hands, engrossed in their own conversation. With the limited people in the cabin it gives his brain room to go on idle. He's staring out the window thinking of Jody.

He rolls through memories of the last few weeks smiling as he flashes to what Jody told him about her mom's comment about him being *the one.* He knows enough about Nita, Jody's mom, from what she has shared, to know she doesn't lend air to being fluffy. He thinks of the power behind her comment. "I'm the one … yes I am, Nita."

My phone lights up with an incoming text. It's from John! "On my way."

I hold my phone with a slight trembling hand excited (and nervous) he's almost here. Even with feeling completely at home with him there's still a nervous excitement about meeting face to face for the first time. Oh my goodness, I am now pacing back in forth in my front entryway. My mom is sitting on the couch. She senses my energy.

"Just be you, Jody."

It's been a long fifteen minutes of anticipation. I feel giddy and playful. My phone rings. I see its John. I quickly answer.

"Hello?"

"Hey you."

Hearing his voice lights me up.

"The driver is having a bit of difficulty finding your place."

"Yeah, it can be a little confusing."

Out of the corner of my eye through the front window I see a black car slowly passing by. That's got to be him.

"I think you may have just passed it."

The car slows down. I cover the phone for a moment whispering loud, "He's here Mom!"

She sits on the couch as I open the door and walk outside.

Inside the car the driver is trying to be helpful. "You want me to back up?" John places the phone down for a moment to answer him. He already has his other hand on the door handle and sees me. He knows the best course of events. The quicker out of the car the better, and the sooner we can be near one another.

"I don't have time, man, but thanks."

Everything becomes slow motion. My heart is thumping in my chest as tears begin to well in my eyes. The door fully opens as John begins to get out. I continue to walk closer to the car, watching (for the first time!) the most beautiful man I have ever seen step out. He has crystal blue eyes and a butt to die for. He's got style, wearing a sheered beaver lambskin jacket paired with stylish jeans and hip shoes.

And, beyond the physical aspect, standing before me the most beautiful part of him, his heart and soul. While in motion, we both click our phones off and continue to walk toward each other in what seems to be slow motion. There are no words exquisite enough to describe what I am feeling. My heart is overflowing with joy and gratitude. Finally we reach one another and without a moment of hesitation we embrace. I let out a sigh as if I have just completed a spiritual marathon and have come across the finish line. It's heaven to finally be in his arms.

He whispers gently in my ear. "There you are." He pulls me a little closer. I respond in surrender. His hands are strong and feel good on my body. Time has officially disappeared. I snuggle my face into his neck feeling the softness of the sheered beaver on his jacket brush across my cheek. He smells so good. "Hi Love. I am so thankful we are here."

Time becomes transparent. Minutes go by without us even knowing it. We stand in my driveway holding one another in the comfort of our love. The silence is broken as he continues to speak gently in my ear. "I have missed you." His voice is twin to a sweet serenade of a long lost home. My eyes begin to mist as I say a silent pray. *Thank you, God.* I pull back slightly and look into his eyes. "I have missed you too, John."

Never in my life have I felt so comfortable with another person.

John says it right out, "I am in love with you Jody."

I blush a little in vulnerability.

"I'm in love with you too, John."

With that his sweet lips reach mine. They are soft like velvet melting me in sheer ecstasy. His hand is on the small of my back pulling me even closer than before. I welcome it as I melt into his arms. As we come to a release I am sent a whisper from those who guide me. I remember one of my favorite sayings by Marcus Aurelius: "Your days are numbered. Use them to throw open the windows of your soul to the sun."

Hello sun.

CHAPTER 50

Our promises create reality

S teve Hardison was correct when he predicted that he would be at my wedding.

Not only is he here, but he is our ordained officiant, conducting the ceremony.

At his invitation, John and I speak our vows, his promises and mine, as family and friends look on from chairs in the open air setting in beautiful, spiritual Sedona, Arizona.

Now Steve turns to John, "John D. Vehr, do you take this woman, Jody Ann Sprecher, to be your lawfully wedded wife based on these covenants you have made to her and on these promises she has made to you?"

John smiles looking straight into my eyes.

"I do."

Steve redirects, turning toward me.

"Jody Ann Sprecher, do you take this man, John D. Vehr, to be your lawfully wedded husband based on these promises you have made to him and these convents he has made to you?"

I smile squeezing John's hands.

"I do."

Steve continues without missing a beat, "John, at this time would you place Jody's ring on her finger as a token of your love for her."

Connor, our nephew and ring bearer fumbles about with

the rings, almost dropping them, but manages a save and hands him the ring. John slides it on. Steve continues, "Jody, at this time would you place John's ring on his finger as a token of your love for him."

This time Connor is holding the ring up for an easy grab. I take it and slide it on John's finger. As we stand face to face, tears in our eyes, we beam with joy.

Steve finalizes the ceremony, "By the authority vested in me by the state of Arizona, I pronounce you, John D. Vehr, and you, Jody Ann Sprecher, husband and wife."

The guests break out into a roar of cheers as John grabs me and lays an oh-so-wonderful kiss on my lips.

And as the months turn to years, our love continues to grow.

I reflect on my journey. What is the lesson for me in all of this?

I could easily get confused. The story could be misunderstood. It *could* look like the lesson is about finding the right man. Like Snow White singing, "Someday my prince will come."

No, no, no. It's deeper and truer than that. The lesson for me was about awakening to the beauty of the journey itself. The real happy ending to this story occurred inside of me, even before I knew John's name. It was when I realized that every experience along the way was happening *for* me, not *to* me. Even DJ. Even Wade. All part of the learning. All gifts.

And there is something else this journey has taught me: I have learned who to listen to!

The divine voice inside of me, the one I've called God, or my angels, for lack of another word, was always right. And the naysayers were always wrong. And that's how it's always going to be, whether I'm awake to it in the moment or not.

My journey has led me out of living daily in a dark forest of fear and low self-worth. I'm no longer there. I used to believe I had nothing to give. Now I see that was never true. I have many gifts to give, including the gift of me just being me.

You, too, have the same gifts. And if the story of my journey gives you some hope and inspiration, I've done what I set out to do.

Don't ever hesitate to give to yourself. And if you're ever too fearful to do it, remember these words:

Find your heart ... follow it ... and then ... *Just Hit Send.*

"Any time you voluntarily let up control, in other words, cease to cling to yourself, you have an access to power. Because otherwise you're wasting energy all the time in self-defense, trying to manage things, trying to force things to conform to your will. The moment you stop doing that, that wasted energy is available. And therefore you are, in that sense, having that energy available, you are one with the divine principle."

~ ALAN WATTS

My Eternal Prayer

by Jody Vehr

I am light.

I am truth.

I am love.

I am eternal peace.

I am one with my beloved Jesus Christ.

I am warrior for the Lord.

I am one with the Divine Feminine, illuminated by her heart and soul, serving others in healing and awakening by sharing my divine authenticity with the world.

I am perfect vulnerability in perfect protection.

I am masterful in the art of language, creating visionary excellence by way of divine inspiration, opening a space for infinite possibility.

I am the voice of Spirit.

I am the evolution of consciousness.

I am divine intervention.

I am loving service.

I am everlasting wisdom.

I am unwavering faith & courage accepting unconditionally the beautiful promise of my soul.

I am the breathing vibration of conscious communion,
creating pathways and bridges for self-actualization.

I am co-creating reality with the Holy Spirit,
serving in the world as a divine clearing for the
architecture of the future.

I am, by the grace of God, aligning to the
light of infinite consciousness.

I am a master of light.

I am gifted with devoted prayer
as my natural state of being.

I am gratitude in motion, inspiring miracles
in the lives of others.

I am joyously awakened in my Authentic Self.

I am chosen and blessed, with my husband.

I am IN LOVE with my beautiful sexy body.

I am fit, lean and in optimal health.

I am distinctly remembering to forget all
that does not serve the highest good.

I am the living discipline of no complaint.

I am STILL and know I AM.

I am my word. Amen.

Acknowledgements

I find myself bewildered by the fact that in the pages that precede this I pour forth my heart with little hesitation and now as I arrive to the acknowledgements I find myself at a loss for words. Perhaps it's due to my belief that there are no words beautiful enough to capture and express the gratitude I feel for those who have helped and loved me along the way. This list includes, but is not limited to, the following people.

To my beloved husband, John Vehr –

I am forever grateful for you and grateful to God for bringing us together. Our love is an extraordinary gift and blessing. You are the most beautiful human being I know. The way you show up in life is an inspiration. I learn and grow from you every day simply by you being you. You are my best friend, my lover and partner with a smile that lights up my world. I know in my heart we have walked together somewhere beyond time, a destination known only to our souls, and like a beautiful wind kissing the sand of a sunlit shore you came into my life bringing with you a love that has profoundly and beautifully touched me. From your presence, from your love, I have healed and grown in ways I never imagined possible. I thank you for that. I thank you with all that I am for loving me the way that you do. I thank you for sharing your light with me, your life and your open heart. A lifetime is not enough to love you. I am blessed to be your wife. I love you.

To Steve Hardison –

November 28th, 2011, the day I met you and my life forever changed in a beautiful direction. I knew from the moment you entered my universe there was something extraordinary about you and our connection. I am thankful for your ability to listen beyond the words I say. It has opened my world up to who I am. You have a unique way about you that is exquisite. It has brought miracles into my life that to this day still blow my mind. Your dedication to service is one that I aspire to attain someday. You have taken it to the level of artistic mastery. Without you and who you BE there would not be a John and Jody. And since he is my everything, I am eternally grateful to you. Thank you for being a guiding light and for reminding me of who I am when I have forgotten. Your presence in my life is profound. Saying I am filled with gratitude for you doesn't capture the magnitude of what I feel. You have helped to clear my mind so I can see the real me, and much to my surprise I like who I am. You are a blessing to me Steve. And just as a caterpillar is committed to its transformation into a butterfly I too am committed to our work together. I look forward to a lifetime of creation with you. Thank you for being one of my greatest teachers and allies. I love you.

To Steve Chandler –

You are one of the most amazing human beings I know. I thank you with all that I am for your love and devotion in the birthing of *Just Hit Send*. I could not have done this without you. Your presence has been a shining light on the dormant gifts of my heart that will extend way beyond the words written here. You are a master of eloquence that comes out in all that you do and all that you BE. I am blessed to have you in my life. Your gentle strength of presence has calmed the sea of transition and gotten me through some rocky uncertain times. You are inspiration both professionally and personally. Your gift with words is extraordinary and your way of being is a blessing to all those around you. I love you Steve. Thank you for all that you are.

To Drs. Ron and Mary Hulnick –

Cofounders of the University of Santa Monica – I thank you for your loving mastery. I am blessed to have studied with you. What I have received from the principals and practices of Spiritual Psychology at USM has had a profound impact. For the first time in my life I know who I am and see what I can create. Thank you for the gift.

To my mom, Nita Sprecher –

Your love got me through the dark night of my soul. If it wasn't for your encouragement and love I would not be where I am. Thank you for never giving up on me and believing in me when I did not. Without you there would not be *Just Hit Send*. Thank you for being wonderful you, Mom. I love you.

To my sister, Samantha Sprecher –

You have always been my rock. I appreciate the many times you've talked me off the edge of the cliff when I wanted to jump. Your love and support mean the world to me. It has gotten me through some of the hardest times in life. I am so thankful for you. I am blessed you are my sister and one of my best friends. How cool is that? I love you.

To my dad, Jerry Sprecher –

Thank you for giving me the courage to walk the path toward change. Had you not been present with your continuous support and kind words I may not have had the strength to move forward. Thank you. I love you.

To my sister, Dani Marcus –

Thank you for being a light in the darkest times of my life. You were my Ann Sullivan. Without you and the knowingness you had, I don't know if I could have made it through. You are an angel to me. I love you.

To my bonus mom, Sharon Sprecher –

Thank you for being the voice of reason. Without your guidance I may have slipped back down a path I did not want to go. Your encouragement was pivotal for making the change I otherwise might not have had the inner strength to make. I thank you and I love you.

To my sister-in-law, Monica Jean –

I thank you for reminding me of my goodness when I had forgotten. In times of serious doubt you were there with kindness of heart encouraging me not to give up on who I am. I love you.

To my nieces, Zoe and Ella –

Thank you for lighting up my world with your love. I am so thankful for you. And, thanks for reminding me it's not an official wedding until there is a crisis. ☺ I love you.

To my Stepchildren, Talia and Andres Vehr –

Thank you both for graciously accepting me into your lives. I am blessed to have you in my life. I love you.

To Jana Cain, my friend since we were two years old –

I thank you for a lifelong friendship and for always being there through the thick and the thin. I especially thank you for dropping everything at 4:00 a.m. and driving to Sacramento (and for the other numerous times you dropped everything for me) to rescue me. ☺ Your friendship is a blessing.

About the Cover Art
(A Tribute to My Coach)

A description from the artist, Briggs Whiteford:

Entirely vulnerable, she steps off a cliff onto a high wire surrounded by infinite mystery and depth of the unknown.

It requires all of her faculties of balance and presence because, if she looks back, she will fall. She risks everything to follow her own creative journey, even though she cannot be sure of anything but the very next step. She has prepared herself with great skill, courage, and determination to forge her own path. She must take this journey alone except for the elements of the natural world. Wind is blowing from below which lifts her. Stars and moon illuminate the way. A white owl, symbol of divinity, spreads its wings behind her. Are these her wings that she will grow on her journey? This is how she learns to fly.

Briggs Whiteford ~ www.BriggsWhiteford.com

About the Author

Jody Vehr is a graduate of the University of Santa Monica where she received her Masters Degree in Spiritual Psychology with an emphasis in Consciousness, Health and Healing. She is currently the Co-owner and Dream Manager of Timney USA where she assists others in the discovery and manifestation of their heartfelt dreams. She is dedicated to the evolution of consciousness by living the truth of her Eternal Prayer. She lives in Arizona with her beloved husband John Vehr and her two wonderful stepchildren Andres and Talia. They are accompanied by their two Neapolitan Mastiffs named Maisie and Baylee.

Contact Jody at:
Jody@justhitsend.com
www.justhitsend.com

Just Hit Send
The Intentions for the Book

October 2014

(These were co-created with Spirit prior to the beginning of the book birthed on the wind of inspiration.)

This or Something Better for the Highest Good of All Concerned.

I am praying and calling myself forward into the highest realms of light and sound. I am giving thanks for your guidance, wisdom, energy and vision Holy Spirit in the manifestation and creation of the intentions here within and content for *Just Hit Send*. This book is yours God, Christ, Holy Spirit, and Guardian Angels. May Thy will be done.

It is the living Divine intention for *Just Hit Send* to be a book of Spirit, a story of love, and for it to gracefully, by the power of the Holy Spirit, BE a positive worldwide influence facilitating inspiration, possibility and miracles in the lives of all who read it, see it on the movie screen, hear about it or experience it in any form or fashion.

It is the intention for *Just Hit Send* to be a powerful tool in the evolution of consciousness as a worldwide best seller in the written form as a book, in electronic format in a form such as Kindle or Audible and on the movie screen as a nominee award-winning, inspiring movie.

It is the intention for the movie of *Just Hit Send* to be co-created by the best of the best in the movie world, using only the highest quality of everything needed to take it to screen.

It is the Divine will for *Just Hit Send* to be a worldwide award-winning movie, facilitating graceful awakening of others to the truth they are Love.

It is the intention of *Just Hit Send* for Christ and the Holy Spirit to infuse it with a timelessness of Spirit, as I am actively and honorably engaging as Spirit's copilot.

It is my intention to serve as a conduit for the Holy Spirit and for the words written in *Just Hit Send* to be living in the energy of the Light and Truth, moving the reader to ownership, inspiration and connectedness to ones own Self and to the Divine.

It is the intention of *Just Hit Send* to effortlessly facilitate spiritual awakening and to spark divine transformation for the highest good of all concerned.

It is the intention of *Just Hit Send* to flow with God's grace as a poetic messenger of Christ in a way that speaks to the soul and to the mind.

It is the intention for *Just Hit Send* to be a miraculous creation from Source, reading with ease and grace.

It is Divine intention for *Just Hit Send* to be an evocative novel of epic appeal, igniting one's Divine imagination.

It is the intention for *Just Hit Send* to be a clear, concise novel that is enchanting and charismatic, serving the highest good of all concerned.

It is the intention of *Just Hit Send* to BE for the masses, reaching and touching the hearts of others regardless of their spiritual beliefs, their age, their race, their gender or their nationality.

It is Divine intention for *Just Hit Send* to be a heartfelt, timeless masterpiece, translated into as many languages at Spirit deems is of Service for the highest good.

It is our intention for the reader of *Just Hit Send* to BE IN the story, and as they read they may be able to step inside the essence of what the story is sharing and claim it for their own.

It is the intention of *Just Hit Send* to speak to the soul touching others on all level of their being fostering an opening for others to be able to accept and awaken, for themselves, their own divinity, healing and growth in ways they never thought possible.

It is Divine intention for the story of *Just Hit Send* to be of living light, masterfully speaking from the highest realms of Light and Sound effortlessly touching the souls of even the most spiritually unconscious (asleep) beings.

It is my intention to serve *Just Hit Send* as Divine intervention.

It is my intention to surrender to the process of birthing *Just Hit Send* and flow in joy as I receive the gift being bestowed upon me.

It is my intention to be fully centered in my heart, vulnerable and open to Divine guidance, in the birthing process of *Just Hit Send* and beyond.

It is Divine intention to infuse *Just Hit Send* with the timeless blessed insights Spirit has bestowed upon me, and for them to flow into *Just Hit Send* with ease and grace … flowing from the Holy Spirit, to me, then to paper.

It is my intention for *Just Hit Send* to be a blessing in all ways and for miracles of the heart to manifest, deepening my relationship, and others' relationship, to Christ.

It is my intention to fully connect and commune with my Masters of Light and Guardian Angels that Guide me and to fully and effortlessly receive and channel their wisdom and insight clearly and powerfully translating it with grace and ease into *Just Hit Send* for the highest good.

It is my intention to welcome and experience the tears, the laughs, the joy, the sorrow, the awakening, the surprises, the inspiration, the healing all in service to the readers healing, growth and transformation (as well as my own) for the highest good of all concerned.

It is my intention for *Just Hit Send* to be an energetic love note from Spirit, reflecting the depth of the blessings available to us all.

It is my intention to flow in ease, grace, love and synergistic harmony while co-creating *Just Hit Send*.

It is my intention for all involved to be wrapped in the Love and Light of the Holy Spirit.

It is my intention for this or something better to manifest highest good for all concerned… May thy will be done. Amen

About The University
of Santa Monica

Over 30 years ago, The University of Santa Monica (USM) pioneered the field of Spiritual Psychology as a response to a growing global yearning for meaning, purpose and fulfillment. USM's groundbreaking Programs in Spiritual Psychology educate students through the unique and highly experiential process of Soul-Centered education.

Students learn and work with relevant, practical information and skills designed to create experiences that support them in Awakening to the Divine within; or the Authentic Self. As a bi-product of their work in consciousness, students' outer lives transform—they live more fully into alignment of their innate gifts and talents, create meaningful work and relationships, and live more fulfilling lives.

University of Santa Monica graduates have used their transformation in consciousness to transform the worlds of business, coaching, education, parenting, government, law, medicine, media, activism and more.

USM's newest Program, Soul-Centered Living I is a 10-month certificate Program in Spiritual Psychology designed to support students in Awakening to the Awareness of who they truly are and living life from that Awakened state.

Learn more at:
www.universityofsantamoncia.edu

48033221R00173

Made in the USA
Charleston, SC
22 October 2015